Contents

PHILOSOPHY OF THE SOCIAL SCIENCES I:
A METASCIENTIFIC INTRODUCTION

Also by J. O. Wisdom in the Avebury Series in the Philosophy of Science

Challengeability in Modern Science

Philosophy of the Social Sciences II : Schemata

Philosophy of the Social Sciences I: A Metascientific Introduction

J. O. WISDOM
University Professor Emeritus
of Philosophy and Social Science,
York University, Toronto

Avebury Series in the Philosophy of Science

Aldershot · Brookfield USA · Hong Kong · Singapore · Sydney

Published by
Avebury
Gower Publishing Company Limited
Gower House
Croft Road
Aldershot
Hants GU11 3HR
England

Gower Publishing Company
Old Post Road
Brookfield
Vermont 05036
USA

0326212

ISBN 0 566 05027 7

Printed and bound in Great Britain by
Biddles Limited, Guildford and King's Lynn

Preface and acknowledgements

This is a companion volume to my *Challengeability in Modern Science* (Gower, 1987) and my forthcoming volume *Philosophy of the Social Sciences II: Schemata* (Gower, 1987).

I have long subscribed to the greater part of Sir Karl Popper's philosophy of science. In *Challengeability in Modern Science* I have been concerned, however, to add to his philosophy of science an ingredient to do with embedded ontology and weltanschauungen, not only because of their unrecognised importance in natural science but also because of their even greater importance in the social sciences (an area in which the notion of weltanschauung *has* been recognised).

I hold, with Sir Karl, that the structure of the social sciences is exactly the same as in the natural sciences (he holds *not quite* the same in one certain respect) and also the methodology (a term I replace throughout by metascience). But there are confusions about his metascience which arise because of the absence of a full exposition of all his metascientific ideas. (I give but broad outline, not minutiae; these books are not polemical.) The main division that has to be made concerns firstly *empirical theories* (not just empirical laws or generalisations). These are universal and are subject to Sir Karl's criterion of testability through refutability. Secondly, contrasted with these, is the class of historical explanations. *Mutatis mutandis* the metascience of these is similar. In *Challengeability in Modern Science* I have devoted considerable space to this area. This is because, to come to grips with the social sciences, it is essential to hive off from general theories' historical explanations. The reason is that, in the present state of the social sciences, there is very little general empirical theory, and most social knowledge takes the form of historical explanations (also empirical generalisations) which in the other book are carefully distinguished from empirical theories. And it is quite common to find that commentators fail to realise that the natural sciences, too, are full of historical explanations (and obviously empirical generalisations). All this is more easily made plain by making explicit the distinctions that Sir Karl makes and putting them in context.

The conceptual distinctions relating to the natural sciences are drawn in *Challengeability*, to have ready for the present volume. But the present volume is to a large extent independent in that the parallel points are made, without, I hope, undue repetition.

The aim of this book is to set out what I conceive to be the Popperian metascience of the social sciences, put in such a way that the structure of it manifests itself, with emphasis only on basic ideas and without falling back on a multitude of logical refinements.

It is hoped that, as a result, it will be possible to develop further aspects of the philosophy of the social sciences.

This book (unlike *Challengeability in Modern Science*), is intended for beginners, especially with the help of a tutor. Since there is so much in the field that is not at all well known, the book may be of service not only to senior undergraduates but also to graduates and even members of faculty in philosophy and in the various social sciences. Some of it is new. The ultimate objective is to go further.

The work results from teaching the subject — at first unwillingly — for over 30 years at four different universities. At one of them I had the enormous privilege of working with Sir Karl Popper and attending with other members of faculty his famous seminars.

In this area I am indebted for help to Prof. Ian Jarvie, Prof. Jagdish Hattiangadi, Dr Helena Sheiham, Dr May Yoh and the late Otto Friedman. I owe, as always, very much to students; but they were mostly concerned with further development, so I will acknowledge them another time.

As with the previous book, I owe an immense debt to my wife Clara and for mostly the same reasons; and also as before to the publisher's reader, Dr David Lamb. I also wish to acknowledge the work done by the publisher's editors.

The following are reprinted in whole or in part by kind permission of the publishers: Review of Brown, Robert (1983) *Explanation in Social Science*, Routledge and Kegan-Paul, London, which appeared in *Economica*; 'General explanation in history' (1976), *History and*

Theory, **15**, 257—66, now Chapter 5, by permission of publisher and editor.

J. O. Wisdom

Wilmont House
Castlebridge
Co. Wexford
September, 1986.

1 The role of philosophy of the social sciences

While it has not been customary to discuss the role of philosophy of natural science or the role of philosophy of science in general, it has been much more common to go into the raison d'etre of philosophy of the social sciences. Although the targets overlap or are common to the two there are noticeable differences. The audience involved may be the sophisticated layman, the philosopher with a certain slant of interest, including the student, and the professional natural scientists themselves. With the philosophy of the social sciences, however, the main target is professional though the other parties come in. Thus, apart from the interests of other audiences, the need for the subject is widely recognised by social scientists themselves and they frequently discuss the philosophy of their subject — a rarity among natural scientists. So there would seem to be a tacit or even overt recognition that philosophy of the social sciences has a close bearing on the practice of social science itself.

Natural scientists (physicists, chemists, biologists, and so on) mostly have science somehow in their bones; they know what to do and they do it. You might think, then, that there is no need for philosophy of the natural sciences. But even natural scientists run into trouble at times. Every great scientific theory has had its philosophical difficulties, even Newton's because of the idea of absolute space. Even the most modern and successful physics, quantum mechanics, is fraught with philosophical difficulties. It is very strange how this happens but it does happen. That is one thing. And then there is something totally different, i.e. that scientists have several different conceptions of what science consists of. You might think they all would agree on this; but there are some six or eight different contemporary views among distinguished scientists about what it is. Hence philosophy of science has the task of investigating the nature of science. And this is not just an interesting thing to do, out of curiosity; there are important repercussions from the view of science adopted, because scientists may come up with a view that prevents certain problems from being investigated scientifically. This, I think, actually happens in the natural sciences; and therefore it is a potent reason for studying the philosophy of the natural sciences.

Although there is some reason for going into the philosophy of the natural sciences that would affect the sciences themselves, the reason with the social sciences is much stronger. Though mostly natural scientists have science in their bones, it is hardly ever so with social scientists. With the social sciences of psychology, anthropology, sociology — economics apart — there is for the most part no body of *abstract explanatory laws and theories* (even false ones) to constitute the solid central core of the subjects. Nor are there clusters of *specific problems* that would constitute a subject. Thus there are some extra-ordinary gaps in the procedures of these sciences which require the philosophy of social science to investigate. Perhaps, moreover, the majority of academics who teach 'social sciences' don't realise they are arguing about 'frameworks' rather than theories or problems. Indeed many do not seem to know what is meant by a 'problem' in 'natural science' — or what is meant by 'scientific method'.

What, then, are the main reasons for the practice of philosophy of the social sciences? There are many.

For ease of reading I have confined the chapters to central topics, while subsidiary matters, even though important, are relegated to appendices to chapters. I am also hiving off certain time-honoured (and also important) topics which belong to the philosophy of social science and its classroom lore, and making of them a separate section at the end of this chapter.

We turn now to the central questions.

1 The difference in nature between natural and social science

It is an old issue whether the social sciences are the same in nature as the natural sciences. The difference was particularly emphasised in Germany and perhaps by the German language, which distinguished between *naturwissenschaft* and *geisteswissenschaft*. The issue here can be expressed briefly: on the one hand, there is the conviction that scientific knowledge is unitary, with an innuendo that there can be no other kind of knowledge. On the other hand, there is an intuitive sense that social knowledge is somehow different, at least because of the peculiar difference between the subject-matter of the two fields — for human beings, whether as individuals or in society, seem to be so wholly different from objects in the world of nature. This is a very significant issue, I would think, but it is scarcely possible to discuss it a priori, at any rate in the hope of reaching any decisive conclusion. The answer would seem to lie in the kind of knowledge that does in fact accrue. Thus those who follow the behaviourists or the conditioning line of enquiry will regard the two fields as the same in nature, whereas those who follow the phenomenological line or its derivatives will regard the two as totally different. But the issue can become much more subtle and discriminating for lines of enquiry in between or which are radically different from both of these. Thus if a mode of enquiry exists or can be found resulting in explanations like those of the natural sciences but doing justice to the special nature of human beings, then the answer for this line of enquiry would also be that the two groups of sciences are the same in nature.

2 The difference in method between the natural and social sciences

There is no *accepted method*. If you inspect the social sciences you find several curious features about their metascience. (i) They often imitate the natural sciences — but the inessential features of these, producing what I would call a parascientific imitation — by adopting a policy of measuring, observing, experimenting, collecting data, etc., which can play an important part but are not characteristic of the natural sciences. (ii) Another common activity is proving the obvious. (To give an example of this, I attended a psychology conference where a paper was given about remedial procedures adopted in a high school to help some pupils who were doing rather badly, and the testing of these. The author devised psychological tests to find out whether the remedial exercises were effective; and it was shown that they were. It seemed to me, however, that a teacher could tell without any such tests whether his pupils were improving or not. It is rather like inventing an instrument in the natural sciences, such as the balance, to tell you whether lead is heavier than wood. This, then, seems to me to be an example of dealing with trivia. It is striking that such a thing can occur at all; it is unknown in the natural sciences.) (iii) A sophisticated form of vacuousness occurs when hypotheses, attempted explanations, are really put forward apparently as they are in the natural sciences, to account for certain phenomena in the social sciences; the work of explanation is carried out appropriately; and the hypotheses seem to provide information. However, if you look at matters closely, you may see that the phenomena thus explained are things that you would expect anyway, even in the absence of the proffered hypotheses. A theory that has any value in the sciences is one that produces unexpected results; the phenomena explained should not occur if the proffered explanation is false. This kind of fallacy is rather a trap, because it is less easy to spot.

On the other hand there are many arguments on the market which add up to the contention that the social sciences are fundamentally different in nature from the natural sciences — for example, that in the social sciences you cannot measure, you cannot experiment, you cannot generalise, and things of this sort, all of which are faulty if you examine the situation. But the point being made is important; for if the social sciences are different in nature from the natural sciences, then you have to think twice about how you should proceed, what your methods should be. So here again is a question you have to go into very closely to see whether in fact these contentions are true. If they are, you have a major problem on your hands. (If they are not true, and if the method is the same, you also have a major problem on your hands, though for another reason.)

This equally significant or possibly more significant question of method has already been touched on in the opening discussion, but more explicitly it comes to this. Is it possible to pursue the social sciences with the same methods as are used in the natural sciences and, also, if this is possible, would any additional new or unique method be necessary to add on top of those? Now this issue is the subject of a long-lasting dispute which of course is still unresolved, and therefore a very living issue indeed. It is by no means a pedantic question; for one's attitude to the answer will determine one's procedures of research, the kind of research that would ensue, and whether the social sciences so conducted would be fruitful or not. There is even strong reason to suppose that backwardness in the social sciences has been due to a number of confusions, even among the main social scientists, about this particular matter. The question here is more significant than the foregoing one because the answer to the question of the nature of the social sciences will tend to hinge on the results ensuing from the choice of methods or the attitude towards method. There are several reasons why this matter is one of the most important. The social scientists who do not discuss it unwittingly take for granted one particular answer to it, which, by reason of not being explicitly thought out, is all the more powerful in its influence upon their thinking and research. There is nothing sacred about classification and if the reader wished to run these two issues into one he would be welcome to do so.

3   Are there ultimate limits to the kinds of explanatory entities?

We might suppose that the areas of the social sciences are different because *persons* enter into them. The natural sciences are concerned with inanimate objects and even animate objects, but not minds or persons. This may seem to hive off the area of the social sciences and make them entirely different. It would provide a concrete and specific reason for thinking that the area is quite different from that of the natural sciences and that each needs a different method of study.

A comment may be made on this point straight away. Biology is concerned with something new over and against physics and chemistry, namely the living organism. By parity of reasoning, it must be fundamentally different from the other natural sciences, and will therefore have to proceed along lines of its own. This, however, is not so. Hence, if biology, which has something so very markedly new and different in it, namely living organisms, is not different as regards method from the other natural sciences, there is no striking reason to suppose that the social sciences dealing with persons have to have a different method either. They might be different, but the reasoning does not show that they must be.

The idea of the ultimacy of persons, and to great numbers of western thinkers it sounds good sense, means that it is impossible to go beyond the human individual as an explanatory entity in accounting for individual and social behaviour; and of course, if so, this would impose corresponding limits on the level of explanatory theories that would be possible in the social sciences. In the natural sciences it is possible to have a theoretical explanation and then to have another level of theoretical explanation behind, above, or beyond that one, and then it is possible to go above that level as well. If the limitation indicated here were valid, this would not be possible in the social sciences and, indeed, there are influential thinkers in several schools that believe this. The contention has the look to most westerners of being self-evident or a priori, but it is difficult to see how it could be proved or disproved. One way, however, in which it could be shown that kinds of explanatory entities or the kinds of explanatory theories in the social sciences go beyond the level of the individual human being would be to *produce* a satisfactory theory that in fact does just this.

4   Implications of the social scientist/observer standing outside society

It is widely maintained that, when studying society or indeed individual people after the manner of the natural scientists, the social scientist is ipso facto placing himself or withdrawing himself *outside* the group or outside the context of the person he is studying. And it is contended that therefore the social sciences cannot be done in principle in this way because an unreality is introduced by placing the scientist/observer outside when in fact he is one with the people he is studying — that he is making an abstraction of himself and indeed an abstraction of the society studied. Put in this form a highly interesting question is raised. It is a specific form of the earlier question (2), because it raises a question of immediate import for social anthropologists. They meet the question in the raw in that they have to become participant observers: that is to say, they have to split themselves into two, being on the one hand observers outside the society studied, while at the same time living in the society as one of its members. The question is perhaps met to a fuller extent by psychoanalysts, who have to remain outside their patients while at the same time recognising that they share the same stresses and conflict as they do. Looking back over these various questions, we see that some of them are not susceptible of immediate discussion but will depend on the outcome of others or of empirical investigations. In fact the basic one is (2), concerning the difference in methods, if any, between the natural and social sciences; but following close behind this is (4), because it is fairly new and at least at first sight presents some difficulty. It may be noted that (2) and possibly (4) *are susceptible* of being discussed on their own merits as metascientific questions. If they can be dealt with, then the next most important question is the nature of explanatory theories, which is a form of (3), and this might possibly help to answer the earlier question about whether metascientific enquiries or the philosophy of the social sciences can prove to be the source of new questions.

Failure of the social sciences

We may turn now to the failure of the social sciences, insofar as they have failed to come up with answers or significant contributions or discoveries. This failure has indeed been widely felt among the social scientists themselves and has led them to adopt one of two metascientific policies and to concentrate on the question of method, which is, of course, a question in the philosophy of science. First, they have succumbed to the temptation of imitating slavishly the processes of the natural scientist, which have been largely misunderstood. In this way they have followed what I would call a parascientific approach — in other words a poor imitation and not the real thing. Since this has not paid off, others have attempted an opposite procedure. They have abandoned the procedure of the natural sciences. In other words they have tried to 'go it alone'. Now it is worth interjecting that this would be quite admirable if it worked. In broad terms, what we want of

6

science is a body of explanation with clear steps in the entire procedure of explaining, such that anyone with the necessary background of knowledge of the subject and sufficient intelligence can follow the process of explanation and give his rational assent to it. No one has succeeded in coming up with a new method for the social sciences that satisfies this broad requirement. Two attempts have been made. Marx tried to provide a holistic or historicist or social determinist mode of explanation in the social sciences (which is undoubtedly different from what is to be found in the natural sciences), but the difficulty is that there does not seem to be any way of testing the results, in other words of deciding in the last resort whether they are to be accepted or rejected. The other approach may be called intuitionist, and is the one followed by most modern psychiatrists, for example. It may have a spiritual ancestor in Weber. The process consists of having an intuitive insight into the nature of people and of social groups. This we must applaud in that one does require intuitive insight; one cannot work without it. But if insights conflict there is no way of settling the dispute. So again, there is no objectivity or ways of giving rational assent.

Between these two poles the social sciences have floundered and they do not seem to have tried the alternative of following the traditional procedure of the natural sciences. Oddly enough there is one, and to my mind only one, instance of a serious attempt to do this, and that is by, of all people, the man who is generally regarded as the least scientific, namely Freud. His explanations are of a high level of abstraction, potentially of great explanatory power, and have all the marks of candidates for being explanations in the sense of the natural sciences. His explanations have so far not reached this stage, because adequate methods for testing them have not been devised or tried out. But at least he is a social scientist who has attempted to follow the classical procedure and very nearly succeeded in doing so. Let us turn lastly to delineating the types of problem areas that arise as a result of all this.

First, we should be concerned with ascertaining the types of explanation to be found in the social sciences, as they are. Then we have to ask whether there are such things as generalisations in the social sciences, whether there are abstract or high-level explanatory theories. Then whether there is a limit, or, as Popper has put it, a 'ceiling' to explanations in the social sciences due to the fact that the social sciences are concerned with *persons*, for it might seem impossible to go beyond an explanation in terms of persons. And further, there would be the question whether some sort of social deterministic, historicist, holistic explanation is possible. Again, there would be the question whether ultimate explanations in the social sciences are entirely individualistic, to be explained in terms of individual persons alone without reference to groups, or whether some group factor (or even a compound of both) must come into the picture. We should further have to investigate whether the existence of personal freedom of the will is compatible with the existence of social science law. We have to consider the question of the different role of values in relation to social science explanations. And in connection with the last question there is a very general question of framework: whether society is to be looked upon in terms of a framework of social function, historical origins, and traditions and whether some or all of these form a necessary feature of the pattern of all explanations in the social sciences.

For this it is plain, first, that the social sciences are at present in a curious position of being confined largely to establishing a framework for carrying out their investigations rather than actually carrying out the investigations themselves. This is an anomalous position. The natural scientist is not in this position. He does not have to be trained in general procedures or methods of science. He learns the details of the methods on the job, the problems are clear, he knows how to tackle them, and he carries out the task. In the social sciences, however, not only is that not the case, but there is no agreement on the general procedure of how the social sciences should be pursued at all. In other words, the entire question of the philosophy of the social sciences is at the centre of the stage; and the central questions are wide open and without a universally accepted answer. And lastly, whereas in the natural sciences the questions are usually clear and the problems understood, in the social sciences for some reason the problems are obscure, and a great deal of spadework of a preliminary kind has to be done before proceeding to formulate and make clear exactly what the problems are. Most problems are alluded to in vague descriptive terms but not made specific. The task of carrying this out is a specific task in the philosophy of science. For all these reasons the philosophy of the social sciences must for some time to come remain central in helping to get the social sciences off the ground.

Other questions in the philosophy of social science

The scope or limits of the social sciences   It would be natural here as in other enquiries to raise the question whether all matters of human nature and of society can in principle be dealt with by procedures in science, that is, by the social sciences. We shall, however, meet this question in a more specific form later.

Havoc to science due to free will   The possible existence of free will, which does not enter into the natural sciences, may well seem to make a fundamental difference. For if in the social sciences we consider people, and people exercise free will, we do not know what they will do next as individuals, nor do we know what groups of people will do next. Hence there can be no orderliness and hence restricted science.

Again, a comment is appropriate. There is an exaggeration here. Modern natural science does not, since the turn of the century, presuppose determinism any longer. There is a certain freedom of play and there is a randomness underneath phenomena that used not to be supposed to be present, yet you do in fact get regularity of laws. There is an unpredictability in the behaviour of subatomic particles; there is a randomness in the breakdown of radium atoms; there is a peculiarity in the impossibility of measuring precisely the position and movement of fundamental particles. Yet none of this disturbs the possibility of having regular laws. If this is so, freedom of the will need not prevent the social sciences from being scientific and presenting some sort of orderly picture either. It has long been known that insurance companies can give you very accurate information, say about how many people are going to die at the age of 41. Now nobody knows beforehand whether John Smith is going to die at the age of 41, but an insurance company can tell in the mass what proportion of people are going to, because the individual differences are all swamped statistically by the large numbers, exactly as in the natural sciences. No one knows who is going to go down a certain subway entrance in New York on a certain Saturday at one minute past two, but the transport authorities know how many people to expect at a certain rush hour. So you can get regularities and understand them in the social sciences even though you do not know the details about the fundamental units, exactly as in the natural sciences. So the possibility of free will need not disturb the picture. Still we can see that it is necessary to go into such questions, and therefore the relevance of philosophy of the social sciences.

The uncertainty of scientific knowledge It is almost universally recognised in the natural sciences that scientific knowledge cannot in principle attain unto certainty. This has been a long drawn-out battle but it is apparently over (though one can never be sure that dead horses may not be flogged again and revived in a stuffed form). While fallibility may be entertained in fairly large measure among social scientists, it is probable that there are certain schools that still hanker after and believe in the possibility of certain knowledge. But it seems hardly worth discussing such an attitude, at least until one is presented with a modicum of examples or a serious case to consider.

The nature of social science There is undoubtedly some difference of interpretation of the nature of social science and this is a highly significant matter. But, like the question of scope and limits, it hinges on questions or specific or ultimate ingredients (such as people) in society.

Science as a rational enterprise Whatever aspects of this matter may be relevant in the field of the natural sciences, different ones might be relevant to the social sciences, to do for instance with subjective and individual reactions, whether these constitute an integral component, and whether the role of values constitutes a limitation upon the rationality of the enterprise. In this context, however, the discussion becomes one about the role of the subjective, the role of the individual, and the role of values.

The demarcation between science and non-science It might with some plausibility be held that there is a fairly sharp demarcation between science and non-science so far as the natural sciences are concerned. In particular, it might be held that there is a sharp line between science and commonsense. The answer to the latter is almost certainly yes-and-no; in certain respects the two are quite different and in certain other respects they are continuous and similar. However, there would be a far greater temptation in the social sciences to hold that they were in large measure identical. For there would be many to maintain that the social sciences are non-science in the classic sense of the natural sciences. Nonetheless the specific issue here does not seem to be the same as the similar question in philosophy of natural science; for here it would be a question whether all social knowledge is included in social science.

Can philosophy of science raise new scientific questions? This is a very serious question, both for the natural sciences and for the social sciences. Traditionally it has been regarded intuitively without discussion as carrying a negative answer. Indeed there is perhaps good reason in both fields to think that a positive answer is the right one. It is hardly susceptible, however, of explicit discussion. The way to answer the question in the affirmative is to produce examples and these can only be arrived at by long and advanced work; possibly of a new kind.

Values Further, there is the notion of values. In the natural sciences you do not have values; in the social sciences you do. People have aims, they value some things more highly than others; cultures, groups, and so on all have certain values and these enter into the picture of the social sciences; and this may appear to make them fundamentally different from the natural sciences. Nonetheless, values can be an object of scientific enquiry like any material object.

One point, however, needs clarification. Consider applications of physiology, e.g. to the human body. A doctor, and to some extent a physiologist, have values which come into the science. A doctor is concerned with processes that make you better and not processes that make you worse. A physiologist is sometimes concerned with the same objective (although more typically his focus is neutral, and concerns, for example, what happens if you inject adrenalin into the blood stream). (Physiologists *could* be concerned with what would do harm. Thus the

Nazis deliberately injected substances into people's veins which they knew would cause violent death. Whatever long term positive value they may have thought they had in mind was in the short run a value on the negative side.) Thus values may appear to enter into the natural sciences or at least into their applications.

However, the values involved in the natural sciences are the ones for which we intend to use the natural science in question. In the social sciences this can be so also, but typically the values that enter in are the values that the object of study has, namely people and society. Thus values enter in as part of the object of study. They may also enter in as part of explanatory theory. They do not enter into the natural sciences in either of these two ways. But, if we can regard values in the social sciences as object of study or as concepts of an explanatory nature, there would seem to be nothing in the nature of values or in the role they play to prevent the social sciences from being treated like the natural sciences and from being pursued by the traditional method of the natural sciences.

The reader may be interested in an extremely good article-review diverging from the present approach by Fay (1984). Useful discussions will also be found in Papinean (1978) and in Thomas (1979).

Appendix 1: The notion of fact

Let it be supposed that the deepest problems of the social sciences concern the operations and changes in society, the broad influences of society upon the individual, and the influence of the individual on society. Let it be supposed, further, that the nature and method of the social sciences are indeed identical with those of the natural sciences. We are nonetheless confronted with some interesting differences. There are some peculiar preliminary questions which do not seem to arise in the case of the natural sciences — at least they do not arise there as a matter of course. In the natural sciences we do not begin with a concern over the nature of a scientific fact or a natural fact, a fact about the natural world. This may be a sophisticated and important question with which one comes to grips at some time or other but is of little urgency. With the social sciences, however, the position is different.

In physics, it is a fact that water boils, that planets are brighter than stars. In biology it is a fact that if you put weedkiller around you will destroy flowers or grass in the vicinity. There is nothing peculiar about this. After a long haul of philosophy of science, one begins to realise that even phenomena of this sort have a certain complex structure. It takes a lot of theory to give an account of boiling or to discriminate between the planets and the stars or to understand the process of killing a living organism. Whereas to begin with we have looked upon them as mere matters of simple observation, as something we had only to open our eyes to look at and record, we have come to the point of regarding all facts, even the most commonplace, as *theory-impregnated*.

To disregard this does little or no harm at all in the natural sciences, for no facts, even by being theory-impregnated, prevent us from forming explanatory theories.

Moreover, there is something hard-headed about *fact* in natural science — in particular physics. A fact, however theory-impregnated and open to challenge, is theory-impregnated on such a humble level compared with the high-level theories that function as explanations. Here is, perhaps, the nub of the matter where a contrast with the social sciences appears. In the social sciences, a fact is simply not hard-headed. At any rate, it is not hard-headed in anything like the same degree as one in physics. Let us try an example. Suppose you get into a bus and spit in the face of the driver. The passengers will gasp or make protests, the police will be sent for, there will be questions, you will perhaps be taken to a police station, maybe even charged. Some of those present may take it very calmly and write you off simply as mad, because your action would be so unaccountable. In such a situation there are two sorts of phenomenon which are so closely connected as to be essentially the same thing. The first concerns passengers, expostulations, police, law, charging — these all take a civilisation, a culture, a society — that is, something *social*, in order to understand them at all. They are not facts in the hard-headed form apparently found in the natural sciences, e.g. if you spill water it runs downhill. In the second place, spitting in the face of the driver is a social factor which has little or nothing to do with water pouring out of one vessel, namely one's mouth, and making an impact upon another object, namely a person's cheek. This last point brings out the difference perhaps more sharply, in that a *social fact* would seem to be a sort of fact about a fact (or a social fact about a physical fact). The physical fact that the water comes out of a tube called 'your mouth' and lights upon a surface called 'the other man's cheek' is per se totally unimportant unless it has a social meaning. If a Martian were to visit the Earth, it would have to be explained to him whether this was a way of paying the fare, or showing friendliness to the driver, or a way of being insulting. He could not know unless he was well-versed in the ways of the society he was visiting. He might have come from a planet where the physical situation was much the same — where water runs downhill and water boils and so forth. But he could not know of the *social significance* of the physical fact.

Now this situation might seem to suggest at first sight that social facts have, so to speak, something subjective about them. At least they seem not to be purely objective in the way that physical facts are. It is an objective fact that water boils at 100 degrees on Earth or on Ma̷ or anywhere in standard conditions of pressure etc. This fact may depend on physical conditions, but it does not depend on the attitudes of human beings. Social effects might, on the other hand, seem culture-relative, and apparently lack objectivity or reality in themselves. Indeed there is some truth in this. In the vast majority of cases a social fact is culture-relative at least in the sense that it cannot be understood apart from the culture in which it occurs. Nonetheless, given a certain cultural structure, a social fact is objective for that culture, and is in no sense arbitrary or subject to alteration at will by any group of people within that culture.

It is, perhaps, possible to go even further. While the meaning of the social fact may vary from culture to culture (in that the same physical performance might have a different social significance in two different cultures), it may be possible to uncover some general social feature relevant to all cultures. Consider the following phenomenon for example. A musician is playing a violin before an audience. After he has concluded his piece, the audience indulges in the physical performance of expelling breath through closed teeth which we call 'hissing'. Now in some Anglo-Saxon cultures this is a sign of contempt, while in some Latin cultures it is a sign of strong approbation. Even though there is nothing in common between the meanings of these two social facts, the physical fact of hissing is, in one culture, a social fact indicating approval, and, in the other culture, a social fact indicating disapproval. We can see that the social fact involves *evaluation* and it also involves *intention*. The intention should express a meaning and possess a purpose. The question might now arise whether there could exist in the social fact anything devoid of evaluation or devoid of purpose. For simplicity, we may here leave out the notion of value because in this context we are concerned not with *high* or *esoteric* values but simply with valuations in the sense of preferences. (So far as we have purposes, we have preferences and values in this sense. We may even take purpose to be the wider concept, in case there should be purposes which we pursue even against our preference.)

If we seek actions devoid of social purpose, the first kinds of examples to occur to us would be these. You might think of idly rambling across the fields without the idea of going anywhere in particular. It is analogous to one or other of the many forms of doodling people may indulge in when they are daydreaming. Again you might indulge in something quite positive and deliberate such as going upstairs to look at the sunset. These two classes of human actions would in a certain significant sense not be social facts. There would be a social factor involved of course, because we should be unlikely to look at the sunset if we had not grown up in a society that took an interest in such things.

13

ould not even doodle unless we were societal human beings.
they are not social facts in the significant sense relevant to
ences in that they do not concern other people or groups
ven so, we have to be careful about excluding them,
f the factors in this sort of activity may very well become
...act in certain circumstances. Thus, if someone began to view
the sunset and then made a habit of it, it might very well have repercussions upon the life of other members of the family (which could
be true even of doodling). If rambling across the fields was carried out
in such an absent-minded way that one did not notice that one was
walking on the corn, there would be social repercussions. A very simple
example of this sort can be found in heedless action, e.g. throwing away
a paper bag in the country, which in some places produces 'litter' and
even social desecration of the countryside. Apart from this qualification,
then it might seem that social facts should be taken to be intentional
and to have a relation to other people as individuals or as groups.

If all this seems reasonably straightforward, we must now touch on a
much more difficult question, namely, can there be a class of social
facts that are, at least ostensibly, not purposive or intentional? Lately
the thesis of situational individualism (and some of its cognates from
other sources) strongly emphasises the purposive or intentional character of social facts. This important though complicated doctrine lies outside our scope; but roughly what this means is that all social activity is
to be explained primarily and in principle in terms of the decisions,
actions, intentions, aims of individual persons — in opposition to the
holistic view that social wholes have aims over and above the aims of
the individuals that compose them. So far, the doctrine would imply
that all social facts are purposive or intentional. However, the doctrine
has a further component: social activity is to be explained in terms of
the actions of individuals not only primarily, but *also* in terms of the
unintended by-products of those actions. Clearly, unintended by-
products are not purposive or intentional.

Thus here we do seem to have a class of social facts that are not
purposive or intentional.

The whole matter may be illuminated by considering Durkheim's
(1938) important discussion of social fact. For Durkheim, two characteristics were important. The first requirement for a fact to be social
is that it should be general throughout a given society, i.e. it should
belong in a society in its own right independent of any particular individuals. Thus a cheque is redeemable by cash at a bank, no matter who is
given the right to cash it or even if no one cashes it. In the second place
— this characteristic is to be added if the first one is already satisfied —
a fact that satisfies this condition in order to qualify as social requires
it to exercise some degree, however small, of constraint on individuals.
Thus a cheque limits the payee to an amount entered on the cheque

and bars him from cashing it at a hospital or a police station. (True, physical facts such as the weather can also exert a pressure, and this may have social repercussions, but the physical fact need not have any, whereas social pressure is intrinsic to social fact.) Such facts, moreover, are objective relative to a given society.

It seems likely that Durkheim would have regarded some social facts as purposive or intentional but probably not all. The cashability of cheques would be purposive or intentional; the death rate would not.

'Objectivity' for Durkheim contrasts of course with 'subjectivity'. It is 'subjective' if one man thinks a certain girl pretty and another does not; it was 'objective' for the Victorian era that a girl must not spend a long time alone with a man. But 'objective' does not mean that a social fact is physically constituted throughout. Thus the cashability of cheques is not physical like the openability of a door. True, a cheque is written on a physical piece of paper (though a recent invention enables a cheque payment to be made by pressing a series of knobs on a computer in the outside wall of a bank on inserting an identification card which is analogous to a signature); but a cheque is not inherently a piece of paper, it is a social operation carried out, from its invention by Lloyds to the present day, with the help of a piece of paper — just as rapid transit is social though it needs the aid of trams. So the 'objectivity' of a social fact is not dependent, or conceptually dependent, upon any physical materials on which it may be conveyed. The 'objectivity' consists in the general recognition of a social fact by a community and in its not being subject to local alteration.

'Objectivity' so described might also be expressed in terms of 'social meaning'. A blue light blinking over a bread shop has no social meaning; a red light along the canals in Amsterdam has. But plainly this way of putting the matter amounts to the same thing.

There is a widespread sense among certain groups of sociologists that objectivity is a misguided aim. Such an attitude appears to be held on three main grounds: it takes the vital pulse out of sociology; moreover in important areas of our social world it is impossible to arrive at the social facts with accuracy or even approximate truth; and lastly social facts thus viewed have no infusion of values. These, however, are problems — problems to be faced. They do not refute the reality of social facts. It is up to those who agree with Durkheim about objective facts to revitalise sociology. The very real difficulty of establishing the social facts in certain areas is an important challenge, for it may reasonably be maintained that without them we should lack all base with which to assess any sociological exploration whatsoever. And, while it is most important to come to grips with value-impregnated social facts, it is equally important to recognise the possibility of another class of social facts that are value-free. The upshot of all this is:

That social facts are not commonly so general as natural facts.

That social facts are not intelligible in the same way: a natural fact is intelligible from the terms of a physical theory used to describe it; a social fact in addition usually needs an understanding of the culture of which it is a part. Some social facts are emphatically culture-relative.

That nonetheless, and because of this, a social fact does possess a certain generality.

That usually a social fact imposes a (commonly mild) restriction upon people.

That a social fact has meaning or intention and purpose.

It may be that there are some absolutely universal social facts.

It may be that there are some social facts that are not intentional or purposive.

While many social facts are value-impregnated, it may be that some are not.

Appendix 1.2: The notion of value

At first sight the concept of values seems to be divorced from that of preference because in its commonest use value tends to be equated with high or esoteric value. Let us begin with preference.

A man may prefer to go short distances by train rather than by bus or he may prefer a hard mattress to a soft one, and no doubt a list of such likes and dislikes could tell us something fairly appreciable about the man's character. But we really do not know much about him unless we know something more than this. For instance, we want to know how much these preferences or likes mean to him. This involves coming to grips with what he is prepared to sacrifice to have them, retain them, or not lose them. We must, of course, distinguish at this point between preferences that are a means to an end and preferences that are ends in themselves. A man may prefer a train to a bus simply because it gets there more quickly and the value turns out to be something different from what we might have supposed, namely time-saving, avoidance of boredom, or some such gain. On the other hand, a man may prefer travelling by train because he enjoys it better. However, we may press him with some questions about why he enjoys it better and we can get answers at least part of the way; he may say that he can look out of the window more easily and enjoy the countryside or read more easily. So here again it would seem that the preference is a means to an end. Nonetheless the end is differently related to the means in this case. Time-saving is an end promoted by train travel and is not a feature of travelling by train as such. Looking out of the window and reading are readily built into the nature of train travel as such. Sources of enjoyment are, in effect, part of the nature of the thing preferred. We might therefore agree that enjoyments are values.

Such values, however, might just be placed under the heading of pleasures. If we know a large number of the simple pleasures that a man indulges in, or tries to satisfy, we undoubtedly know something about his character, but we really do not know a great deal about it unless we know how much store he sets by these pleasures, that is, how much he is prepared to sacrifice to have them and maintain them and prevent them from being lost. In large numbers of simple cases a man will be disappointed if one of these 'simple pleasures' is precluded, but he will not take the matter too seriously (if it happens to be difficult to get to the railway station he will perhaps shrug his shoulders and go by bus). In certain cases, however, he will go to inordinate lengths to make sure that he will not miss some such pleasure — he may do an inordinate amount of overtime to save up for a week's holiday lying on the beach by the sea. We are here confronted with the question of how much what the man seeks *actually means to him*. Or, in other words, with its *worthwhileness*.

It is at this point, I think, that the distinction begins to emerge between preferences concerned with enjoyments and things that are meaningful or worthwhile. It may be legitimate to think of the former as values; but they are so only in a very modest sense; and what we tend to think of as *value* enters the scene only when we enter the realm of what is *worthwhile*.

Restricting the notion of value, then, to what is meaningful and worthwhile, we need to bear in mind: that values may be purely individual since they vary widely from person to person; that they may be shared and even come into large groups with some variation between groups; and that they may be universal to mankind. One further distinction must be drawn and that is between subsidiary and ultimate values in any such system, with, of course, many gradations in between.

For definiteness let us collect one or two specific examples. A man may have as a meaningful objective the value of being muscularly very strong. He may not be able to say at all why this is important to him, but it may be as meaningful to him as the value a group may attach to rendering excellent service, such as providing reliable watches. Again, all human societies, however different their ideas of justice may be, maintain that justice exists as an ideal, and hold, according to their perception of it, that every effort should be made to realise it.

These several forms of values are equivalent to motives or determinants of human action. It is not of course that the values themselves are causes. It is the commitment to a value that operates to get things done or prevent things from getting done. This point having been made, however, there will be nothing really misleading in speaking of values as determinants. It is likewise clear that they are cognate with purposes. One of the merits in utilising the category of value rather than that of purpose or of motive or some other is that it may make it slightly easier to adhere to the discrimination between individual, group, and universal categories. Moreover, it seems easier to form frameworks of values, whether for individual groups or mankind as a whole; this may, of course, be done for motives or purpose also, but it falls in place more smoothly with values. The concept of value moreover has the advantage of underlining the notion of meaningfulness of states of affairs, actions, or whatever. It must be apparent that whatever conception of social structure we eventually reach must depend upon such notions as value and meaningfulness.

While one of the great classical questions about values is whether they are man-made, a more directly important question in the social sciences concerns the *influence* of values on mankind, whether as a whole, on some human societies, or on individuals. (Other questions concern the possibility that our values bias our researches; and the possibility that all our researches have our values embedded in them. Newer questions are whether societal values *evolve,* and whether argumentation somehow alters values.)

In sum, the concept of values, used so widely, does not seem too hard to designate. It concerns not satisfactions as such but rather their worthwhileness. This is so, irrespective of whether value is common to mankind, is limited to a group, or is purely individual. The concept of value underlines *meaningfulness* in human affairs.

Appendix 1.3: The notion of social reality

Being given the notions of social fact and values, we have to consider the notions of social reality, culture, and so forth, in particular to see which has the wider catchment. We want to know roughly what sorts of special entities make them up: in other words what the notions refer to.

It seems clear that social reality is the widest social concept of all. It includes social fact, custom, tradition, articulated law, social beliefs, taboos, values, and social institutions. Nor should magic and myth be left out. If the physical basis of society would have it that man is what he eats, the constitution of society amounts to man's being what he supposes (no matter whether his suppositions are false or true). Thus social reality includes everything that man supposes. We may conveniently divide the things that man is obliged to do or permits himself to do, on the one hand, and, on the other hand, the things that by custom he refrains from or by law (including religion) is overtly forbidden from doing (and in the latter connection, of course, there arises the phenomenon of violation).

Thus social reality includes what is done or allowable and what is not done or disallowed.

In addition, social reality includes the machinery for implementing or preventing these things. The machinery may, of course, be entirely individual: a man may spear a fish to get his lunch. This is not, however, the interesting part of the machinery. The interesting part of social machinery consists rather of social institutions (and of course of lesser forms of social practices that would hardly be called institutions). One could say that social organisation includes the sum total of ways of getting things done that are sanctioned or ordered and preventing other things from being done either forbidden expressly or contrary to custom.

However, interestingly enough, social organisation and its various constituents have a reality or solidity more than one might have expected at first sight, though they seem to be entirely intangible. Suppose that one infringes on some component of social reality. In some cases this will lead to physical consequences for one's physical body. In an extreme case, one's body may be put behind bars, and in a less extreme case money may be taken away from the guilty party, or perhaps some belonging such as a cow. In another kind of case, however, there may be no penalty exacted, but there may be social pressure which, however subtle, will act, in the last resort, upon that man's body. Thus if he has not shown sufficient respect to the head man of the village on a certain occasion, he may find that when he goes to the pub people turn their backs; though he may not be refused a drink, he may find that he is unable to have a conversation. In other words, something that he wants to do will be interfered with. Moreover he may have to do something that he does not want to do such as making amends by submitting some sort of apology to the head man. Indeed, things may go so far that a man's wants may actually alter.

In coming to grips with the basics of society, it does not seem, however, that the notion of social reality by itself can explain anything in depth (though it can explain a great deal at the guidebook level). What is necessary is to realise its existence and not to underestimate it. One could, however, say that the basic problem is to explain the *existence* of social reality, its systems, and its change.

How does 'social reality' relate to 'culture'? 'Culture', as used in an undefined way in social writings, is quite useful for general purposes and it is doubtful whether there is anything to be gained by giving it any very precise use. It would seem that 'culture' fundamentally hinges on scales of values or frameworks of values and refers to different levels of values, so that the concept is a simple shorthand way of referring to these. The simplest procedure might be to conduct enquiries in terms of value-systems and frameworks of values where any kind of precision is required, but not to eliminate the use of the notion of culture in broad contexts.

Thus it seems as though both 'culture' and 'social reality' are rather informal in their uses. They both seem to designate the same field, the entire field of social entities and relationships; 'culture' puts more emphasis on 'values'. The notion of 'social reality' gives sufficient emphasis to a basic feature of culture — its intangible nature. 'Social structure' is another closely connected concept, somewhat smaller in scope: it refers roughly to the more or less permanent components of a society; but a brief account of the concept is well-nigh impossible. For purposes of social explanation, it would seem that the most important concept is that of value (perhaps in a context of social structure).

Only a brief mention is appropriate here of the great questions to which 'value' gives rise. Perhaps the most central ones are whether there are any values that are universal for all mankind in all ages, whether there is any way of ranking and comparing them, whether there is any way of criticising them, and whether there is any criterion for their existence.

In sum, social reality designates hosts of entities that are just as 'real' as trees and clouds, tables and chairs, mice and men, but differently real in that their reality is intangible, including customs and values, institutions and social habits — what is allowable and what is not, together with the socially accepted ways of bringing about what is allowable and what is not as well as ways of preventing them.

One last consideration: is there any criterion for the reality of social 'realities'? The following may, perhaps, be offered: a social construction is real, if and only if there are occurrences, of more than one kind, that can reasonably be interpreted as effects attributable to that construction.

References

Durkheim, Emil (1938), *The rules of sociological method,* University of Chicago Press, Chicago.

Fay, Brian (1984), Naturalism as a Philosophy of Social Science, *Philosophy of the Social Sciences,* 14, 529–42.

Papineau, David (1978), *For Science in the Social Sciences,* Macmillan, London.

Thomas, David (1979), *Naturalism and Social Science: a post empiricist philosophy of social science,* Cambridge University Press, Cambridge.

2 Commonplace explanations

It is well known to social scientists that all sorts of explanations are sought in ordinary life taking the form of answers to questions: how do you account for, how do you explain, how did this happen, why did this happen? Social scientists are aware on the one hand that there are various types of explanation used in answering these questions. The ease with which many of them can be answered induces a sense that much is known in the social sciences about behaviour. The variety, however, is misleading, for the knowledge involved has a certain triviality, and is even an index of failure to attain more fundamental knowledge.

It is, however, worth distinguishing some different kinds of questions that are asked at the level of ordinary life or 'kitchen' knowledge; it can be done very briefly.

'Why is dinner late?' 'Because there was a power-cut.' 'Why is dinner late?' 'Because cook dawdled.' 'Why did Scott's expedition to the South Pole end in disaster?' 'Because of a concatenation of circumstances — everything went wrong that could go wrong.' 'Why do you drive along this road, which is longer?' 'Because there is a rule closing it to heavy vehicles.' 'Why was Franco kept alive with special drugs?' 'Because it is a moral duty to preserve life.' 'Why was Franco kept alive with special drugs?' 'Because extra time was required for political manoeuvre.'

It will be observed that these are historical in nature and also that they mostly involve explanation by particulars. One of the commonest types of explanation sought is a fairly simple account of the circumstances that led up to an event which we find somewhat surprising. Such events, which may be called the enigmas of history, cease to be enigmas when a satisfactory account is forthcoming. Thus when Costello announced in Ottawa, completely out of the blue, that he was taking Eire out of the British Commonwealth, this took the world by surprise and in particular the United Kingdom government — that government had had no previous intimation that this move was going to be made or even that it was being tentatively considered. The exodus duly took place, adjustments were made, the United Kingdom government expressed regret but accepted the situation and helped to effect the transition. For many years no explanation was forthcoming — hardly even a rumour; however, in the end it was rumoured, apparently on good authority, that the Irish Prime Minister had felt himself insulted at a British Commonwealth gathering by a British Governor-General, whereupon he made an unpremeditated announcement to the press. Years later some evidence emerged that the decision had been taken previously by an inner cabinet. In such an example the solution to the enigma, whether the first account or the second or a combination, consists of describing the events, when they can be unearthed, that led up to it. While there may be further questions that we may wish to ask, there is no doubt that such an account is an essential part of an answer to any further account. Whether or not it contains any historical laws, hypotheses, or generalisations, it mainly consists of social facts, these are what are said to be described[1], and the description supplies the account required to dispose of the enigma.

It will be evident that the account just given is typical of at least some form of historical explanation. This would be where an event is explained by an event that happened at some previous time. But it will be seen that there are other historical explanations very nearly the same as this. Consider some historical questions which take the form of asking 'why?' Often this is simply a grammatical difference and they amount to the same question. The typical kind of 'why?' question in this context is simply a request for explanation which is available to some people but not to the questioner. This is all that makes the question different from the enquiry about an enigma, for an enigma is one that is an enigma to almost everybody (apart from a few who may have inside information not available to the public).

Questions that ask 'how?' can be exactly the same, if they mean, 'How did it come about that so and so?' However, questions that ask 'how?' can be different if they mean 'in what manner?' Thus 'how did Cleopatra die?' in the first meaning is to be answered by being told that she put an asp in her bosom. In the second meaning the answer would be, 'she died right royally as one descended from a line of kings.'

So far we have a historical answer reporting a prior event, which may answer 'how?' or 'why?', and secondly an adverbial answer.

We may now distinguish a further form of question asking 'why?' in the sense in which it means 'for what purpose?' Thus, 'why did Truman drop the atomic bomb?' may be given the answer, 'in order to effect a drastic shortening of the war and save many American lives'. Here we are referring to the point, goal, or purpose involved.

A further variation under this heading emerges from a question that asks what process or mechanism is involved in bringing about a certain result. Thus if we ask what was the process by which the House of Lords was divested of its last real sanction, the answer would be that the Prime Minister of the day, namely Asquith, persuaded George V in 1911 to agree to create a great number of new peers, who would vote as Asquith wanted them to in the House of Lords, unless the House itself willingly agreed to relinquish its traditional power; and it did so, rather than have a whole lot of new peers thrust upon it (whereupon it would lose its power anyway). This answer not only explains an enigma, or describes a circumstance for which some of us do not know the answer, but also describes the manner in which the result was brought about.

Let us turn now to another type of question raised under the form of asking 'why?', namely in the sense of 'for what purpose?' Here there is a whole crop of questions that are almost identical; in fact they differ only in being slightly different from a grammatical point of view. It is possible to ask 'for what purpose?', it is possible to ask 'what was the intention?', 'for what reason?', 'what was the motive?' No doubt subtle differences between these may be unearthed in certain specific cases on the fringe but by and large they all amount to the same thing; thus with the question 'for what purpose did Truman drop the atomic bomb?' we have as answers, 'the *purpose* was to shorten the war', 'his *intention* was to shorten the war', 'his *reason* was that it would shorten the war', and 'his *motive* was to shorten the war'.

One or two points should be made in connection with these questions. One concerns yet again fullness of formulation. Social scientists find themselves hampered because in common life many questions of this sort are incompletely formulated. One hackneyed example in the literature is the question, 'why did a certain man go into a shop?', the answer being 'to get some tobacco' — this was his goal, this was his reason, this was his motive, this was his intention. Now questions of this sort have to do with the notion of an action. We are concerned with the intention behind an action, the reason for the action, the motive for an action, the purpose of an action. What needs to be made clear about this particular example of a man going into a shop is that the action has not been fully articulated. We may certainly wish to know why the man went into the shop, but this could be expressed by saying 'we want to know what his action really was'. His action was that he went into a shop to buy some tobacco. The significant question for the social scientist does not begin before that, even if it begins at that point; you require to know the purpose, motive, reason, intention involved in going to buy tobacco. But we are not concerned with the metascience of unspecific situations that do not amount to being action at all, even though these are quite important in ordinary life and in the law courts. Such questions and answers are subspecies of historical investigations because they are answered in terms of a purpose that the man has entertained in mind prior to carrying out the action (even if he has not deliberated upon it).

It is quite clear that such questions and explanations are common in ordinary life and of great practical importance, but in the metascience of the social sciences. the interesting questions arise only afterwards, that is, when we raise further questions about these answers.

A contrary fashion became widespread through the later philosophy of Wittgenstein. He introduced a philosophy of language which was a linguistic form of British empirical philosophy. That philosophy, whether as given by Locke 300 years ago or by Russell from 1911 onwards, rested on a basic axiom, that the only objects of experience we can have knowledge of are our sensations — all else lay *outside* the circle of our sensations and are problematic or perhaps even a myth. Wittgenstein likewise adopted the basic assumption that anything we customarily say in our ordinary speech makes sense ('Why did he put his knife and fork down in two parallel lines?' 'Not because he believed Euclid's geometry and was an opponent of Einstein's relativity theory, but, he may say, out of good table manners'); but anything we say *outside* the circle of our ordinary way of communicating would be unintelligible, i.e. could not be said, because it would violate the conditions of ordinary speech. For this kind of reason, Wittgenstein in his later philosophy appeared to think that all matters of social behaviour could be answered in terms of answers to questions of intention or purpose or even a motive or some such. This was an extreme view amounting to the doctrine that no further question could be asked, should be asked, or was in any way relevant to the social sciences. The short answer to this is perhaps that since the more significant questions in the social sciences were not considered in this approach to philosophy, no reason has been advanced against them — only an implied taboo of meaninglessness.

In connection with this type of explanation there should be mentioned other factors with a strong family resemblance to those already described, namely explanation in terms of dispositions or habits or 'rule-following'. Thus the explanation of a man's lighting a cigarette is force of habit, or his disposition to smoke. Such explanations are in practice of great importance in social, medical, legal, and other fields; but the metascientific questions arises only afterwards when we wish to know the reasons in another sense, namely the explanations of the

24

dispositions or of the practice of rule-following. Wittgenstein regarded all social behaviour as rule-following. Thus, in speaking, a person follows the implicit rules of grammar. In catching a bus, a professor is following a number of rules to do with the fact that he has to reach the university at a certain time in order to give a lecture, in order to carry out his obligations. Here once more the metascientific questions that arise concern two types of questions, namely, 'what is the explanation of the rules?' and 'why do people accept them?'

It is clear that these questions concerning 'why?' in the sense of asking for purpose, disposition, rules, etc., are of practical significance but of no metascientific interest.

Let us now revert to the notion that a great deal of social knowledge is involved in the possibility of answering all these types of question. This is of course true; there is social knowledge in the sense of social know-how. The point has already been made that the metascientific significance begins only afterwards and not at this juncture. But a further point must be made here, namely, that this is not an achievement peculiar to the social sciences. An exact parallel to many of the above situations can be found in the natural sciences. Thus if we asked what circumstances led up to the phenomenon so-and-so, how did so-and-so come about, why did it happen, what cause led to it, what process produced it, what underlying condition was involved in it, all these have their parallels. Thus we may want to know how it was that a fire started in a room with no readily combustible materials, what led to an unexpected earthquake, what process led to the collapse of the Forth Bridge, why the kettle which had been left on the fire had a hole in it. The only point that I am concerned to make here is that we have a great deal of common knowledge consisting of materials from natural science which serves to explain many things. We may not be able to answer without technical enquiry about the Forth Bridge or about the earthquake, but we can tell that if we leave a kettle without water we shall burn a hole in the bottom of the kettle. The reason why the huge amount of knowledge which is common knowledge of processes in the world of nature passes unnoticed is that the natural sciences have advanced so far that we possess huge numbers of generalisations, and even reliable generalisations, and a respectable number of fine explanatory theories. In the social sciences, however, there is an almost entire absence of the last, not many formulated generalisations even of a statistical kind, but a large number of intuitively known though unformulated generalisations. The effect is that we are apt to ask whether we really know anything in the social sciences at all. And then we reflect seriously that we do have a great deal of knowledge of a know-how kind. Nonetheless it is a knowledge that we would hardly give a second thought to, any more than we do in the case of knowledge of the natural world, if we had more effective generalisations and especially theories.

There is, however, one respect in which the social sciences seem to have a slight edge, and that concerns our knowledge of human nature and of ourselves and of one another. Just by being human we know very well that other people would be annoyed if they were spat upon, and we do not have to do research in a laboratory to find this out, whereas we do not have the same sort of access to simple knowledge about stones and water. Two comments may be made upon this. One is that it is arguable that we have had to achieve such knowledge in the process of growing up only by the same sort of processes by which we obtained knowledge of the natural world, i.e. that we do not really gain such knowledge by the privileged position of being human. I would not entirely subscribe to this. It is undoubtedly true that merely being human is not enough; we have to find out by learning processes of some sort, nonetheless the fact of being human enables us to employ those processes, or at least to supply us with conjectures, which we should find much more difficult to obtain otherwise, even though we might in the end be able to obtain them. The other comment is that if this does give the social sciences a slight edge over the natural sciences, the edge is very slight. The sole gain is a certain amount of knowledge of the category of know-how, and this is not scientific knowledge in the sense of explanation; it is, rather, the material that gives rise to problems, or is the starting point of the search for social science explanations.

What, then, remains that has not been delineated? Two things: one is the question whether there are generalisations, whether either universal or statistical generalisations really do occur in the social sciences. And the other is whether there are explanatory theories. These are large matters that must be separately gone into at length.

To put together the main points made:

The idea that we (we, ordinary people) have a great deal of social science knowledge comes down to a blend of the following: most of what may appear to be such is social know-how; this, though genuine knowledge, is not unique in being social, for it is exactly paralleled by our physical science knowledge or know-how, e.g. concerning boiling kettles, and throwing stones at glass; it consists of generalities of human life; it is thus at the triviality end of the spectrum of general knowledge; it therefore constitutes, not so much explanatory knowledge though it possesses this to a small extent, but social phenomena requiring social science explanation — it is not the end of social science enquiry but the beginning.

Such commonplace explanations are historical; and the anatomy of historical explanations, as we shall see, shows something of the variety of types it contains. It also shows that, for the most part though perhaps not always, the social science laws involved are trivial. This is of no importance when they are simply service-laws in certain contexts;

but it is detrimental to our understanding of the social sciences if we look on them as typical of social science knowledge. Further commonplace explanations are nearly all concerned with explanation of particulars by particulars — again excellent, but misleading if it leads us to regard the social sciences as concerned solely or mainly with explanation by particulars with no ambitions towards general theory.

I wish to turn now to a different source of confusion. If we look on a scheme of explanation of particulars by particulars not as relevant solely to history but as giving us allusions to social science knowledge of a general kind, we confuse science (i.e. theoretical explanatory science) with technology. This confusion is widespread enough so far as the natural sciences are concerned, but most people will grasp what theoretical explanatory science is about if it is expounded with examples. But it is harder to get this across where the social sciences are concerned, probably largely because of the embedded outlook that the aim of the social sciences is to better the lot of man. This is the task of social technology. It is not the task of theoretical explanatory social science. Now the use of technology brings about a *particular* change. Hence the schema for technology is closely linked with the schema of historical explanation — both lead to end-points which are particulars. That is why, I suggest, the emphasis on commonplace social science knowledge is likely to support — and also receive support from — the idea that social science is essentially social technology. By getting this clear we see that there is a place left open for societal theory.

Note

1   It is worth drawing attention to a distinction made by Robert Brown between 'reporting' and 'describing': he says quite correctly that this procedure is not strictly speaking describing but reporting; and I would accept that the above account was a report consisting essentially of the fact that Costello regarded himself as insulted and took a certain action in consequence. 'Describing', as this occurs in novels, poetry, and so on, would be a much fuller activity bringing in all sorts of details of the event which are not really relevant to the report required by the enigma. The description, for example, might involve the frown on the Irish Prime Minister's face; but all the report requires is that he felt insulted and took offence. However, although this distinction seems valid, the term 'describe' has been used in philosophy of science for a long time, though unwittingly directed towards the material of a report, i.e. it has been used as a synonym for the term 'report'. This

may be a misuse of the term as it is employed in everyday English but no misleading consequence has ensued; so it is permissible to use either term according to circumstance.

References

Brown, Robert (1963), *Explanation in Social Science,* Routledge & Kegan Paul, London.
Popper, K.R. (1964), *The Poverty of Historicism,* London.

3 Generalisations in the social sciences

Theoretical knowledge in the social sciences is scanty. Faced with this situation, two opposed approaches have arisen: one, that in the social sciences we should copy the methods of the natural sciences; the other that the social sciences should 'go it alone'.

Let us engage those groups who maintain that the social sciences are sui generis and that their methods are quite different from those of the natural sciences. It is not that these anti-scientific groups deny the possibility of explanation in the social sciences altogether; they hold that the social sciences go their own route, but this entails that there is nothing fundamental in common between the two domains.

Anti-science groups have to hold that the social sciences fail to contain either generalisations or theories, since these are basic ingredients of the natural sciences. Here we are concerned with the question whether there are or are not generalisations. The basic work of elucidation here has already been done by Popper in the first chapter of his *The Poverty of Historicism* and carried through with complete lucidity and cogency; it has been well explained by Robert Brown (1963) in his textbook *Explanation in Social Science.* However, in both cases the treatment has been associated with themes slightly extraneous to them.[1] But the presence or absence of generalisations in the social sciences must be settled in its own right. I therefore think it necessary to run very rapidly through the main points involved detached from other issues. The reader shall also consult Gellner (1956) and Donagan (1974).

We need to be explicit about the scope of the term 'generalisation' and make it clear that it should cover not only universal generalisations — it is widely questioned whether there is any universal generalisation in social science at all — but also to cover statistical generalisations. It must be emphasised at once that this is wholly in keeping with the natural sciences, where statistical generalisations are nowadays, if not the rule, very nearly the rule. It would be a mistake to claim that all generalisations in the natural sciences are statistical; they can be put in this light if we are determined to interpret all physical phenomena in terms of statistical physical theory, but this is itself a *theory* — a metatheory — and we do not in all circumstances have to use it. That would be going to one extreme. But even if we go to the other extreme and maintain that most generalisations in the natural sciences are universal, we still have to admit that there are many significant generalisations that are statistical, even without falling back on the statistical interpretation of physics. Thus it is a statistical generalisation that the normal temperature of a human being is 36.9°. Again, in physics the half life of radium is statistically 8,000 years; thus it cannot be too strongly emphasised that in the natural sciences statistical generations are perfectly scientific.

What needs to be added, however, is that there is a feature of universality that attaches even to statistical generalisations: thus the statistical generalisation about radium holds not simply of this planet or some particular period of life on this planet but of radium everywhere. Anti-natural science groups deny the existence of generalisations whether universal in this way or any other or statistical.

I will now run through half a dozen arguments, the tenor, result, fallacy, and grain of truth in all of which come to the same thing.

Experimentation

It has been fairly widely felt that the social sciences cannot really be sciences because they do not have experiments. This argument presupposes that experimentation is a sine qua non or part of the essence of science; with such a presupposition it is natural that the social scientist should try to imitate what he conceives to be the proper procedure for the natural sciences, namely to carry out experiments. It is very easy to see, however, that there are many domains in the natural sciences where experiments do not take place at all. Astronomy is perhaps the most obvious. The metascientific point is that, when we seek to test a theory or a hypothesis in science, we need to do so as carefully as possible and therefore a controlled experiment is highly cogent if we can conduct one; but failing that, an observation that arises in some way other than in an experimental situation is quite good enough; experiment may or may not produce a refinement, and the experiment is only relevant when it does produce a refinement. So in short, experiment, though beneficial where possible and relevant, is very far from essential.

This part of the argument against the scientific nature of the social sciences is clearly based on a misapprehension. On the other hand it is simply false that there is no experimentation in the social sciences. Experiments on kinds of leadership in groups consisted of the following. In all groups a task was set. In one group no leader was assigned at all by the experimenter. In another a permissive leader was openly installed who would give guidance but not go against the wishes of the group. And in the other a leader was put in to play the deliberate role of a dictator. Each group was then observed to see which one produced the most effective solution to their task.

An interesting rider can be added on this matter. There have been events in our history which have been deliberately brought about but not with the explicit aim of experimenting, and yet the results in retrospect can be interpreted in terms of experimentation. In 1936 Keynes published his theory about some of the relationships between inflation and monetary policy. The old idea was that a government should balance its budget. It was a consequence of Keynes's theory that in times of depression a government should underbalance its budget so as to leave more money in the pockets of the population to help circulation and effect recovery, while in times of inflation the policy should be to overbalance the budget, that is, to take more in taxes than the government would actually spend. When the Second World War broke out Keynes was given a room in the Treasury (I believe without either title or salary) and he ran the finances of the war. War always produces inflation and Keynes sought to control it by having the Chancellor of the Exchequer overbalance the budget, not just in a small way but on a huge scale. This proved so effective that the depreciation of the value of the currency over the period of the war was only one-third (nothing like comparable to the large inflations that have taken place since). Now an action taken like this is not an experiment, which is something designed to test a theory, but is a policy designed to achieve a certain objective in real life. Nonetheless, when we look back on the whole matter, we may, if so minded, reinterpret the situation as if the action adopted by Keynes was an experiment. And this of course occurs in the natural sciences too: thus when oxygen was first given to a patient who had difficulty in breathing for the express purpose of giving him ease, this may be reinterpreted afterwards as an experiment. Thus if Keynes's measures were introduced not to control the currency but to test out whether the currency would be controlled, that would have been an experiment; and the practical operation can be interpreted as equivalent to that experiment. Similarly oxygen given to a patient to help him may be interpreted as an experiment to test its conjectured efficacy.

A further example of deliberate experimentation would be that of the Harlows in bringing up monkeys away from their natural mother on wire screens with bottles of milk attached, one screen consisting of bare wire only and another, for comparison, covered by a woolly cloth.

Too much should not be granted to retrospective experiments. The truth in the charge of lack of experimentation is simply that there is *not very much deliberate experimentation* possible in the social sciences. Here we must distinguish very sharply between the metascientific point that experimentation is in principle possible and in fact does really occur on occasion and the recognition that in practice there is not and cannot be very much experimentation. The significance of the distinction is that the possibility of experimentation is enough to show that the methods are not inherently different, so far as this ground is concerned, in the domains of natural and social science. The practical difference, on the other hand, shows that it may in many cases be more difficult to do social science or to do it with the same sort of rough accuracy as we expect in the natural sciences. The natural sciences are very far from being exact, but the paucity of experimentation may mean that the social sciences may well be for ever still less exact. Even this limitation, however, would not apply in situations where experimentation is hardly called for.

Novelty

It has sometimes been maintained that there can be no parallel between the two domains because there is no novelty in the world of natural science whereas novelty is everywhere to be found in the social world. Obviously, however, the properties arising from putting together complex molecules produces novel results; and even more strikingly, scientists of recent decades, who invented and synthesised new elements, were certainly producing something novel in the field of natural science. This argument is totally uninteresting.

Complexity

There has existed the argument that the two domains are essentially different because of the complexity of the social sciences, whereas the natural sciences are extremely simple. This objection would seem to be rooted in the naive image of the natural sciences as based mainly on such things as the solar system and also perhaps on the fact that in physics laboratories one can isolate certain phenomena in a fairly simple way. To take the first point, it is overlooked that the solar system is not at all characteristic of the physical world; it is in fact a most unusual phenomenon (though there are doubtless many other solar systems like it elsewhere in the many galaxies). That this is the characteristic situation in the world of physics is a sheer myth. Physicists do not often tackle messy problems because they have so many others that they can devote their time to, but consider the following. A leaf is blown off a tree and carried by the wind across a football ground. Ask a physicist to write down the equations of motion! This he simply cannot do. Physicists could not cope with such complications. Yet such motion is the kind of thing that is characteristic of the natural world. Moreover, in the early days of the study, say, of electricity or heat, the phenomena were so messy that physicists could make very little of them and there was no uniformity of approach between researchers in one university and another. This is somewhat like the situation in the social sciences today. It may be that the natural scientists have the edge in that they can produce neat isolated experiments with only a couple of variables involved; and that is usually beyond what it is possible for social scientists to do. On the other hand it may be simply that social scientists have not yet located the simplicities they could manage and make basic; we should bear in mind that in the field of natural science it was a long time before it was possible to isolate the simplicities.

However, even if it should be the case that inherently the field of social science is complicated in a way that is not characteristic of the field of natural science, this constitutes a difference in degree only. It does not mean that the social and natural sciences are essentially different. What it could mean is that the methods adopted in the natural sciences for coping with complicated situations might be the only ones that could be taken over by the social scientists.

Here again there is no inherent cogency in the argument that social science is sui generis.

Exact prediction

It is the glory of natural science to be able to make fairly exact predictions, whereas this is seldom possible in social sciences. Here again we meet the phenomenon of a faulty image of the natural sciences rooted in a few such natural occurrences as eclipses, which can be predicted with great accuracy. On the other hand prediction in the social sciences is as a rule rough and ready. For instance, it is possible to predict that in time of war there will be inflation. But the degree of inflation can be predicted only within very wide limits. The point is sometimes brought up that nothing can interfere with a prediction made in the field of natural science, whereas untoward events may totally upset a prediction in the social sciences. This claim, however, does not hold. It is predicted that there will be a total eclipse of the sun visible in the South of England from Cornwall on 11 August 1999; but of course if a passing star or even one of our own rockets were to knock the moon slightly out of its present course, that would be the end of this prediction.

Exactness of prediction is relative and not an inherent difference.

Objectivity, validation, and self-fulfilling prophecy

While it is generally held that the methods of the natural sciences are objective and that there is an apparatus of validation, it is widely claimed that there is no parallel to this in the social sciences.

The claim in effect is that examination of a social phenomenon ipso facto alters it, rather in the way that investigating an electron jolts it. Such a disturbance is usually regarded in the world of physics as atypical and at any rate very small, but as general in the social world. Thus, in particular, when a social event is predicted, the very making and consciousness of the prediction may alter the outcome. In extreme cases predicting — publicly — might bring about the prediction itself, which might not have occurred otherwise; or alternatively might prevent the occurrence of the event, which would otherwise have taken place. For example, if the Governor of the Bank of England mentions that he expects the pound to rise, many institutions will be influenced by the announcement to buy sterling, which will make the pound go up. Or, when Marshal Pétain predicted (in 1940) that Great Britain would have its neck wrung like a chicken by the Germans, the effect might have been to stiffen resistance and negate the realisation of the prediction. These are extreme cases. But it is possible that such eventualities might be widespread in the macroscopic social world — as contrasted with the rarity, because more or less confined to the microscopic, in the physical world. It is at least plausible that social observation is a social influence.

It is, however, going rather far to endow the point with generality. It is easy to find examples that are free from such interference. Thus consider the proposition, 'If a government ruthlessly subdues a population there will be revolt.' In applying this law we may have occasion to consider observations of ruthless subjugation and of revolts; and these are not of a kind to be influenced in the way described.

The question may properly be raised, how to distinguish social situations that are subject to influence by observation or prediction from those that are not. In answer to this, I would submit that for all such observations we always have a theory, presupposed, according to which the given situation might be or might not be subject to interference. In the light of such a factor, we consider whether or not there is likely to be interference, and how much interference there is likely to be (so as to allow for it, as far as possible). The existence of uninfluenced social facts is thus theory-contingent. Hence objectivity of social observation is not ruled out.

It is worth adding that without a reasonable measure of objective social observation, suitable for testing social hypotheses, it is hard to see how social science could be conducted at all.

Quantitative generalisations

It is held that one of the glories of natural science is that generalisations are quantitative, whereas this is not so in the social sciences. The first point is that there are areas of natural science that are not quantitative. This has been well brought out by Webb (1944). Moreover it has been rather widely overlooked that even the quantitative areas of physics are sophisticated developments resting in turn upon qualitative investigations. Thus if we wish to investigate the quantitative relations between heat and expansion of metals, so as to get the numerical coefficient of expansion, this presupposes the qualitative generalisation that heat *qualitatively* causes metals to expand. And there are qualitative experiments that (in the laboratory sense) 'demonstrate' the phenomenon. On the other hand, Durkheim's law about suicides is quantitative.

This argument is understandable but it has no punch.

The influence of social theories

Somewhat cognate with the foregoing is the notion that social theories can influence the development of society in the direction suggested by these theories. An obvious example would be that the communistic governments of the world have been brought about by Marx's theory which predicted them. Such a phenomenon may very well occur. Treat a subordinate as irresponsible and you may very soon find you have an irresponsible colleague on your hands. There does not seem to be a parallel in physics; for predicting the behaviour of an electron or the breakdown of radium and so on does not tend to bring it about, or rather the theories about these entities do not affect their subsequent behaviour. Although here we have a more interesting point, its occurrence cannot be very frequent, though some examples, such as that of Marx, may be most influential and widespread. If we are at pains to protect ourselves from this self-fulfilling result, all we have to do is to keep the social theory under lock and key, and not make it available to those people who when influenced by it would help to bring about the developments predicted by the theory. Still, isolation is not always possible; and sometimes social ideas *can* bring about their own fulfilment. The need in such a case, and it is somewhat greater than in the natural sciences, is to estimate the extent of the induced implementation.

Epoch relativism

Even if some or all of the foregoing have begun to lose their grip there is a widespread belief that generalisations in the social sciences, though they exist, hold only in certain cultural settings, historical situations, or briefly in a specific epoch.

This argument again displays a faulty image of the nature of generalisations in the natural sciences. It is often the case that a generalisation holds only for a certain sort of situation. But the usual procedure is to include the conditions in which a generalisation holds as part of its statement (even though in practice this is omitted in overt statements because all natural scientists know the conditions that apply and take them for granted). Thus if a law about the expansion of gases is mentioned, no one bothers to state that it holds only for middle ranges of temperature. But if this qualification is put in, the law would be expected to hold universally. In a parallel way let us consider classical economics. It is quite true that it does not hold now; but if one inserts the conditions of a more or less free market, then theories of classical economics have a universal form; the sole drawback to them is that they can be used only in certain conditions and that they are no longer *applicable*. It is not that they are false; it is simply that they do not apply. But the same is true of a gas law. If one inserts the condition into the statement of the gas law that it relates to a medium range of temperature, when stated thus it is not false near the sun, it is simply inapplicable. Likewise epoch-relativism can be largely, if not wholly, circumvented by inserting the requisite conditions in which a generalisation is claimed to hold.

Holistic approaches

However, there is an entire approach to the social sciences completely at variance with that of the natural sciences; this is the approach of holism, or of what Popper calls historicism, rooted in intuitive apprehension of inner truths and based upon the concept of an inner essence. Popper has linked all the above objections to generalisations and to the applicability of the methods of the natural sciences in the field of the social sciences to this historicist approach. This linkage is misleading, but while Popper is entirely correct that the holistic approach does reject generalisations for all the reasons discussed above, the (invalid) objections unfortunately can all be used on their own (scanty) merits by social scientists who would have nothing to do with the holistic approach at all.

That is to say, while the above arguments are natural to the thinking of the holist or historicist, arguments against holism and historicism as such do not suffice to reject the above arguments, for they can be maintained on their own.

But Popper in fact has launched a two-pronged attack: he has tried to refute holism and historicism by attacking all the above miscellaneous arguments; and on the other hand he has tried to attack holism and historicism directly. It is perhaps questionable whether there is any way in which the latter can in fact be carried out; but a word is necessary on the second prong. To show, as Popper does most successfully, that generalisations exist and are not open to the objections we have gone through above does not invalidate holism and historicism, for the following reason. It would be perfectly possible for a holist or historicist to admit the existence of generalisations but to maintain that these were superficial and unimportant in comparison with the deep truths revealed to the intuitive understanding about wholes and the historical process. These would be his real objective, and the existence of (paltry) generalisations would be in no way incompatible with it.

A word of caution. It should not be thought that the argumentation conducted here succeeds in establishing that generalisations exist in social sciences in exactly the same way as in the natural sciences. To argue against misunderstandings and mistakes does not prove the thesis that those misunderstandings and mistakes were designed to oppose. All that the argumentation does is to weaken the opposition. However, having weakened it and shown that there is no solid ground for opposition, we are in a position to turn to generalisations on their own merits, inspect the notion and enquire detachedly whether there are such entities. Examples in general do not constitute proof, but one example can be proof of a possibility; and all we have to do is to point to the existence of a single generalisation to show the *possibility* of generalisations existing; and this very simply establishes the point at issue.

It is an unfortunate fact that so many considerations of this kind with so little punch in them should have exercised so much influence for so long. It is quite possible that no single social scientist has been impressed by all of them, but many social scientists have been caught by one or two of them. And the barrage of considerations of this kind must have caught a great many in their net. Much damage has been done to the pursuit of the social sciences by misunderstanding of the nature of science.

Appendix 3.1: The covering-law model

It is widely though far from universally agreed that something like the Popper–Hempel 'covering-law' model is required for all historical

37

explanation, which consists in explaining particular events by particular events under the linkage of a generalisation or law (the 'covering' law). Broadly put, this is the view that historical explanation of a particular event, often a current one, is explained by an earlier particular event in deductive fashion only with the aid of a law connecting events of those kinds; the law 'covers' the deductive inference.

Argument goes to and fro about details of the covering law, and about whether it is really presupposed or not, and about whether or not it is logically satisfactory.

The notion was introduced by Popper (1936) and by Hempel (1942), and I call it the Popper—Hempel model. (Popper (1934) virtually gave it even in his first book, for he there depicted the *same* notion for causal explanation, though without mentioning its equal applicability to historical explanation, an identification he made later on.)

Schematically, from the conjectured event h_1, together with the law 'if an event of the type h_1 occurs, then an event of the type h_2 occurs', there follows deductively the event h_2 which was required to be explained. (Popper (1945) sets this out in more detail, and Hempel (1949) formulates it rather meticulously.) I also call it the 'detective' schema. Thus when Sherlock Holmes and Lestrade found a certain corpse, their problem was h_2, a murder to be explained. Holmes told Lestrade that the murderer was well over six feet tall, was red-faced, and smoked a Trichinopoli cigar — so it was only a question of finding the man. Holmes had made three historical conjectures h_1. One was the smoking, with the law that a Trichinopoli cigar leaves Trichinopoli cigar ash. (Holmes was an expert on cigar ash and wrote a monograph on the subject, without, however, taking his doctorate.) The second was a conjecture about the murderer's eye-level, with the law that if a man writes on the wall he does so at eye-level; and there was writing on the wall about 5ft 10in from the ground. The third was that the murderer's nose had bled, with the law (which is hard to ascribe to Conan Doyle, who was a doctor and should not have used a flagrantly false medical law) that if a man has apoplexy he is subject to nose bleeding and is red-faced (the idea being that high blood pressure will show in the pigment of the face and will burst through a weak spot in a vein).

Examples of covering laws from the philosophical texts are not very good. Popper gave an excellent one from the natural world explaining why a certain thread broke. The conjectured h_1 was that a weight of 1kg was suspended from it, and the law was that above a critical tension of ½kg the thread would break. The reason why this example is illuminating is that it reveals Popper's intention that the event to be explained should be a correct logical deduction from the conjectured historical antecedent and the covering law; for the adequacy of the deduction is not always apparent in historical examples offered in the philosophical literature.

An example from history would be b_2, the outbreak of World War I, explained by b_1, the support required by the Austrians which was given by the German Government (more particularly, if we wish, by the warlords in the cabinet who gained the ascendancy), covered by the generalisation that, if a country that needs support in order to go to war obtains that support, it will start the war envisaged.

These examples illustrate Popper's ideal of a complete *deduction* of the b_2 from the conjectured b_1. It needs to be added that the framework does not require that there should be only one single covering law (Dray's (1957) book hinges on the basic assumption that such is Popper's idea). The historical interval between b_1 and b_2 could be a process broken down into any number of intervals each with its own covering law. Indeed the process need not be a chain; it could be a network. There is nothing to preclude such elaborations. Popper himself was obviously just giving a minimum simple framework applicable to the simplest type of case — unrealistic of course as the realities of history go, but there is nothing theoretical to be learnt from making the framework more complicated and realistic.

Applied with plausibility to the most boring simplest cases, we can see the plausibility of having generalisations or laws as presuppositions. We take for granted, for example, that if a cigarette falls on dry wood shavings there will be a fire. If an ultimatum is not complied with, war will follow. If peaky mountains are steam-rolled by an iceberg they will be rounded. If an army does not receive full support it will not fight well. If we keep weak characters out of harm's way we shall avoid making them worse. If we avoid situations that encourage disrespect for law or society, then we shall decrease the number of court hearings.

I would, however, broaden the model slightly. From Popper and also Hempel one gets a picture of 'linear' laws in which historical laws form a chain and one sees history as a number of causal chains from the past to the present. This is obviously oversimplified and in fact what we have is interlocking networks. Thus, the laws presupposed need to be enlarged from being linear to being web-like laws. This modification involves no alteration of principle and I fail to see that there is in it anything that either Popper or Hempel need object to. Nor is it to be suggested that they took a naive view of history in putting forward the causal chain model — they may even have been thinking in terms of a network. But a chain can be part of a network, and I think they may have been only attempting to deal with a metascientific point in the simplest possible way.

Should the examples and the relevant model here considered strike the reader as paltry, not measuring up to the richness of history as written by the greater historians, the point should be admitted. But the paltriness does not mean that the questions which treat only of such particular events are unimportant. Thus it is of moment to know that an air crash was due to a faulty bolt, or to understand the web of circumstances leading up to the sinking of the *Princess Victoria* between Stranraer and Larne. Moreover such questions can be of considerable human interest. In any case, however, they open up matters of metascientific significance.

Now, these minor considerations apart, for they do not affect the standing of the covering-law model, what of its opponents? The model has been rejected by a number of philosophers: the lead was taken by Dray (1957), and he was followed by Donagan (1959) and by Danto (1968). In answer, Hempel made some concessions that did no damage to the notion of 'covering law'. He enlarged the conception to include statistical laws (Hempel 1965), and he also recognised that laws or generalisations may be general statements about a particular, e.g. 'This dog always barks at the postman' (Hempel 1963, p. 342; cf. White 1969, pp. 89f; Murphey 1973, pp. 76f). The covering-law model has also been strongly defended by Goldstein (1962, p. 181), and in more detail by White (1969, Ch. 2) and by Murphey (1973, Ch. 3).

What, then, are the considerations that strike Dray as rendering the model faulty or even unthinkable? Dray would seem to be animated by a sense that the historical explanation of an event is to be located in the rationality of a person's intentions and actions, which he considers have no reference to covering laws. Such a view would seem to be restricted to the purposive components of the explanation which takes no notice of covering laws. But, of course, no one on either side of the issue thinks of covering laws as being consciously considered by the historian. And no argument has been advanced to show that they are not logically *presupposed* (even Mill conceded that inference from particulars was impossible without a general licence). Of course Dray might have intended his arguments that the model is neither necessary nor sufficient to refute the claim that the model is a presupposition. Sufficiency, as hardly needs to be argued, is too strong; for an accidental interference factor such as a passing star could completely upset the relation between an event and the historical antecedent explaining it. But necessity is what is at stake, and Dray apparently gains his point by mistaking Popper to mean that a linkage between an event and its historical explanation must consist of a *single* covering law; whereas of course there could be any number of laws forming a chain of linkage.[2]

However, although the covering-law model has been successfully defended in large measure over a number of points,[3] it should be emphasised that there are one or two (not more) loose ends.

It is worth mentioning the oddity of the strategy of proving an event to be neither necessary nor sufficient (as a way of showing that the event has no role). Coitus is neither necessary nor sufficient for pregnancy. Apart from a few primitive communities, where the denial of the connection is in fact questionable, does anyone conclude that coitus has no bearing on pregnancy?

Can 'covering laws' cover?

Now most examples of covering laws do not permit of exact deduction of h_2; they look 'near enough' or need just a small auxiliary connecting link. The reason is not far to seek: it is relatively easy to retrodict specifically; but in the forward direction, many outcomes are possible. Consider h_2, the American hostile reactions that ensued due to h_1, the levying of taxes as of right by England without American representation; here the covering law is that, if the superior governing body acts autocratically to the extent of provoking great resentment, then revolt is to be expected. Strictly speaking, the hostile reactions are not deducible. There are various possibilities. Those imposed upon might have thought of some ingenious way of bringing pressure to bear on the autocrat inducing him to desist, of a deal involving some other power by which the autocrat would desist on promise of some attractive gain; or they might have concluded that it was the will of God that they should bear such a burden. Such a looseness in the deduction is mitigated by requiring not that h_2 should be deducible specifically by being covered by a universal generalisation but only that it should be deducible with probability. Hempel, taking a less exacting approach than Popper, is content to have, not a full-blown deductive explanation, but an 'explanation-sketch' (Hempel 1970). A sketch implies a framework that can be filled out if necessary, and points in the direction in which the filling is to be found. Hempel himself seems to have in mind the explanation of very general features of a situation. But if we wish to use his idea for the explanation of a specific h_2, then we are thrown back by the sketch to the position that the cover offered is one of probability. But probability, after all, is fully adequate — provided the probability deduction holds and is not merely a disguised form of vague deduction. A probability framework would be difficult to work out but should be amenable to treatment.

Dray (1957) has argued that a covering law is neither necessary nor sufficient. But he did not argue this for a probability model. If a probability model could be elaborated, it would be sufficient.

Thus the objection that the hypothetico-deductive framework fails, i.e. that the covering-law model fails to provide for a valid deduction of the event to be explained, would seem to be met.

The sole loose end that Murphey (1973—74) considers left in the defence of the covering-law model concerns a defect, which greatly exercised Dray and also Danto (1968), undermining the possibility of a 'covering law' giving cover. It is worth noting that opponents of the covering-law model do not dwell on the positive aspect of the issue, the need for such laws as presuppositions or inference licences to service inference from particulars to particulars. They concentrate on the negative aspect, to show that such laws cannot in fact do the work required of them. The strongest of such attacks, perhaps the only one not so far fully answered, is Dray's argument that a covering law must either be rendered so feature-less as to be incapable of servicing the particulars or be rendered so specific as to apply only to the given particulars. That is to say, the covering law, to work, must be so *general* that it cannot 'cover' a specific event or must be so *specific* that it cannot apply to more than one item.

Thus our dog, Moss, is nice to visitors, but Moss always barks at the postman. The particulars are the event now, namely Moss's barking at the postman, and the explanatory event, namely one day the postman trod on Moss's paw.

Now on investigation it transpires that Moss has not *regularly barked* at the postman — often though not always; he has sometimes just growled. To abridge the matter: he has sometimes bared his teeth silently. So the law is that Moss is always unfriendly to the postman. And this could not service an explanation of barking.

Alternatively, we recall that members of the family have occasionally trodden on Moss without similar results. So we have to say that the covering law is that Moss always barks at anyone he doesn't know who has trodden on him. Then we find that he does not react this way to the doctor; so the covering law now is that Moss always barks at anyone he doesn't know wearing a uniform or who has trodden on him . . . We end up with a covering law that Moss always barks at anyone who has all and only the characteristics of the postman. And this is ad hoc.

The phenomenon that creates this dilemma is the open-endedness of personal and social behaviour — indeed the necessary open-endedness of dispositions. Quite generally the explanation h of the particular e is the *disposition* of h to lead to e. And when the disposition is filled in, to take account of situations when e did not occur, we end up with the dilemma that either the disposition is so emptied that it cannot service h and e or it is so qualified that it can service no others. In both situations we are under the pressure of the boundary threat that the disposition leads to e except when it doesn't. In this a dispositional explanation differs apparently from a causal explanation as this is familiar in laboratory natural science. In the latter case, the exceptions are (apparently) few in number and can be included as conditions in the formulation of the causal law. When a causal law is found to break down in a natural science laboratory, the phenomenon is full of interest and can lead to a new discovery — as when bacteria were found dead in the presence of a fungus (which Fleming 'knew' could not kill them, thus discovering penicillin). One has the impression that the splay of tracks of consequences of causal laws, due to the presence of alternative conditions, is discrete, that the tracks are sharply separated from one another; on the other hand, the tracks of consequences flowing from dispositions seem like the co-ordinate axes in a geometry with an infinite number of dimensions.

The ingenuity of whodunits shows that, when confronted with an explanatory task and very little to guide one, it is impossible to make a satisfactory conjecture about the explanation. And, apart from whodunits, in ordinary life, it is a commonplace that when someone is late home a surprising variety of explanations abound, quite beyond the possibility of conjecture. As Sherlock Holmes said, it is a capital mistake to reason without data (which may incidentally have given ostensible support to people's propensity to believe in induction, to think they must first observe the facts).

Perhaps the answer is as follows. A specific covering law is taken for granted; not assumed as true; it is assumed as a specimen of law that could, and would often, cover or service the explanation from particular to particular; if it were to be found, on challenge to be false, nonetheless it would tell us what *kind* of law would service the explanation and would tell us that *some specimen of that kind* does service it. If some specimen *does* service it, the deductive inference is in order. Now this conclusion holds whether or not the initial covering law is in fact challenged, and whether or not a replacement specimen is in fact found that is *known* to be true.

Should the investigation, arising from actually challenging the assumed cover, reveal the possibility of a totally different explanation, without reaching confirmation of the replacement specimen, then we have an interesting situation in historical research leading to a new view of that piece of history.

Dray's model of reconstructed calculation

The contention that a covering law is indeed necessary rests simply on the fact that it is apparently impossible to explain a later particular, b_2, by an earlier particular, b_1, without a logical means of transition. I understand that even Mill recognised this logic.

Now Dray (1957) thinks there is an alternative, which he calls the *model of the continuous series*; it could also be called the *model of reconstructed calculation.*

Introducing the subject via a mechanical example, Dray considers a car engine that seizes up due to an oil leak; when coached by a garage mechanic in elementary trouble tracing, he learns

that if no oil arrives the piston will not move because the walls are dry; that the oil is normally brought to the cylinder by a certain pipe from the pump, and ultimately from the reservoir; that the leak, being on the underside of the reservoir, allowed the oil to run out, and that no oil therefore reached the cylinder ... (pp. 67–8).

Dray then gives the interpretation that to understand a phenomenon historically is to 'trace the course of events by which it came about' (p. 68); he can now envisage a 'continuous series of happenings' between the leak and the seizure (p. 68).

One notes with interest that 'the oil is normally brought to the cylinder by a certain pipe from the pump'; this statement reads not like an antecedent condition but like a law (and if so Popper exaggerates in holding that trivial laws are never mentioned in historical accounts). But this is a small point of inconsistency and Dray could probably smooth it out.

One notes also the laws at the surface of the account, e.g. if there is a hole in the bottom of a pipe, oil will escape. However, for Dray they play no part, neither presupposed nor silent.

But *what would it be like for one of these laws to be false?* — without recourse to the simple answer of a *miracle.* It would be impossible to continue the story of a continuous series of happenings, if the oil did not escape through the hole at the bottom of the pipe as the law maintains it would. And where Dray (1957, pp. 68–9) adds that the chain of events into which the leak leading to seizure is broken down has to be 'acceptable' to someone, one may wonder on what grounds it might be acceptable; and the only answer would seem to consist of the laws.

Dray (1957, p. 122) offers a somewhat similar account of the great mistake made by Louis XIV of withdrawing military pressure from Holland, as explained by Trevelyan (1938)

> He was vexed with James, who unwisely chose this moment of all, to refuse the help and advice of his French patron, upon whose friendship he had based his whole policy. But Louis was not entirely passion's slave. No doubt he felt irritation with James, but he also calculated that, even if William landed in England, there would be civil war and long troubles, as always in that factious island. Meanwhile, he could conquer Europe at leisure. 'For twenty years,' says Lord Acton, 'it had been his desire to neutralize England by internal broils, and he was glad to have the Dutch out of the way (in England) while he dealt a blow at the Emperor Leopold (in Germany).' He thought 'it was impossible that the conflict between James and William should not yield him an opportunity.' This calculation was not as absurd as it looks

after the event. It was only defeated by the unexpected solidity of a new type of Revolution.

This brilliant quotation certainly looks tailored for Dray: it is not Dray but Trevelyan who writes of Louis' calculation; Dray sums it up as Trevelyan's *reconstruction of that calculation.*

But one would wish to know how Louis could calculate, plan, decide (even incorrectly) without laws? If the law were false that, if a foreign prince/general landed in another country there would be a local war, how could Louis possibly have calculated what would happen if William of Orange landed in England? Planning and decision-taking presuppose laws in the same way as does explanation by a historical antecedent.

The argument for the necessity of covering laws has the same structure as the method of investigating the function of an organ such as the heart: interfere in some specific way with the input to or with the output from the organ and you will discover its function; similarly, interfere with a relevant law and you will discover its indispensability.

I now wish to append some remarks on some critics of the model. Some incisive criticism of the Popper model (in Hempel's form) has been given by Nowell-Smith (1970), who has given the best treatment so far known to me of history as narrative. Apart from a number of good points, he has two main criticisms: the first is that the model has no central connection with what historians actually do, nor can they seek generalisations. I am reasonably certain that Popper would largely agree, and that these aims were not the point of the model (though on occasion the historian does include a generalisation and may very rarely seek them). The point is that the model provides a metascientific framework into which historical narratives and constructions fit. Nowell-Smith, I think, detracts from his lucid and interesting paper by assuming that in the covering-law model explanation is equivalent to predictive power. Now Popper's model has little to do with prediction. (Indeed prediction is only loosely connected with explanation in natural science; it is not a criterion of explanation but it plays a part in providing tests of hypotheses.) Prediction can play a similar part in historical explanation.

Certain points need to be made against Nowell-Smith's version (which he might be able to concede without loss). The covering-law model (at least in Popper's form, whatever might be claimed about Hempel's) does *not* — or does not basically or often — aim at finding general laws; one might find such in Lecky but not typically. Nor does it aim at *prediction.* True, a historical conjecture/interpretation may on occasion be tested by a consequence. Thus there is the attribution of the murder of the princes in the tower to Henry VII rather than to Richard III according to the traditional accusation made in Henry's time and underwritten by Shakespeare. This re-view of history would explain certain oddities such as that the murder charge against Richard did not appear in the subsequent somewhat detailed indictment of him by the House of Commons. But a prediction would help. If the princes' skeletons were found and dated, that would be telling. They *were* found but could not be dated; it was all too short a time ago for carbon-dating, and of course there is the question of identification — we do not have X-rays of the princes' teeth. The covering-law model would be gratified by prediction; but all it aims at is a coherent explanation of the known subsequent events. On this level I am inclined to think that the charge against Richard is in about as strong a position as the astronomical conjecture of visitations to Earth from outer space.

Thus it seems to me that Nowell-Smith's attack misses its target.

Goode (1977) also provides a recent criticism of the Popper model (in Hempel's form), which gives an excellent bibliography of recent writings on the subject. The author prefers, without perhaps quite endorsing, Dray's model; the alternative model to Popper's is essentially Mill's explanation of particulars by particulars. Against both of these the author, like Nowell-Smith, suggests that the real philosophical problem is not explanation but the aims and problem-situations of historians.

This author too seems to me to understand the objective of Popper and others; he seems to think that those who uphold the covering-law model, what he calls the 'regularity' thesis, are urging historians to *seek* laws or regularities (finding them 'of little help to the historian', Goode 1977, 373, cf 381, 382, 384, and he says this explicitly of Hempel, 381), that they take no account of and misconstrue the kind of explanations historians seek. Apart from this there are large parts of his paper that a Popperian would accept, such as his stress on the uniqueness of the historical event (it is not uncommon in controversy to parade, not necessarily deliberately, an array of contentions all would accept and 'refute' the opponent by charging him with denying them). Popper would, I think, be the first to repudiate the idea that historical research should *seek* covering laws, and indeed to point out that particulars occur in the world of natural science and give rise to the same kind of explanatory problem as in (political) history — though often here the explanation hinges explicitly on natural laws known or to be discovered. Popper's model concerns a *logical* point, not a *historical* one.

Having satisfied himself that the Covering Law theory is false, Nowell-Smith (1981), adopting the approach of Dray though in a more sophisticated way, depicted historical explanation as narrative; the narrative, however, is not a single causal chain, but a complex pattern. It will be seen from my treatment of the subject in this Appendix that I too attach great importance to narrative. That is to say, I consider historical explanation, whether of kings and battles or the evolution of the stars, to be basically a narrative. But to this is added the contention that on Popper's model every step in the narrative has to be accompanied by a Covering Law.

Conclusion

The covering-law controversy has the look of being a battle on the periphery with little bearing on the outcome of the war and no repercussions on matters outside, on wider philosophical issues. (This may be a slight exaggeration, for opposition to the model may well be in aid of and stem from a vogue for 'informal' logic.) The question whether there are covering laws seems capable of being answered with a 'Yes' or 'No'. Objections to the model have been steadily answered, apart from a loose end or two, and I have attempted to resolve the residue. And I have tried to give a fresh argument for the need for covering laws.

It is worth remarking that the anatomy dissected in Chapter 4 would still be of account, even if the covering-law model were found to fail. If we should become interested in other possible types of historical explanation overtly involving laws, it would be beneficial to have the anatomy of historical questions depicted above, even if their setting within the model were discarded.

Notes

1 Thus Popper puts the attack on generalisations into the mouth of historicists and holists. In this he is of course perfectly correct, but there are many thinkers in the field of the social sciences who are neither holists nor historicists but who think that generalisations do not exist. This is extremely widespread, and the basic error is of such significance that it prevents social scientists from going on to more important areas of the metascientific enquiries of their field. Robert Brown does not commit this mistake, indeed he opposes it; but while his treatment is wholly lucid, he lists a considerable number of types of explanation side by side as if they were in some way parallels. It is perhaps only a minor defect but it is somewhat misleading.
2 I am indebted to Dr May Yoh for this criticism.
3 There are some useful if elementary papers by Teggart, Cohen, and Mandelbaum (all 1942).
    I do not know whether Nowell-Smith would be able to sustain his position if he conceded the above points (that the Covering Law does not *seek* general laws, or the complaint that this is not how

historians work, and that prediction is not sought). I suspect that without these convictions in the background he would find his position infirm and unattractive. He too should be faced with the question, 'What if a relevant law were false?'

References

Cohen, M.R. (1942), 'Causation and its application to history', *J. hist. ideas*, 3, 12—29.

Danto, A.C. (1965), *Analytical philosophy of history*, University Press, Cambridge.

Donagan, Alan (1959), 'Explanation in history', *Theories of history*, ed. Gardiner (P.), Free Press, Glencoe, Ill., 428—43.

Donagan, Alan (1974), 'Popper's examination of historicism', *The philosophy of Karl Popper*, Ed. Schilpp, Open Court, La Salle, Ill., 2, 905—24.

Dray, W.H. (1957), *Laws and explanation in history*, University Press, Oxford.

Gellner, Ernest (1956), 'Explanation in history', *Proc. Arist. Soc.*, suppl vol. 30, 157—76.

Goode, Terry M. (1977), 'Explanation, Expansion, and the Aims of Historians: Towards an Alternative Account of Historical Explanation', *Philosophy of the Social Sciences*, 7, 367—84.

Hempel, C.G. (1965), 'Aspects of scientific explanation', *Aspects of scientific explanation and other essays*, Free Press, New York, 447—63.

Mandelbaum, Maurice (1942), 'Causation in historical events', *J. hist. ideas*, 3, 30—50.

Murphey, M.G. (1973), *Our knowledge of the historical past*, Bobbs-Merrill, Indianapolis

Nowell-Smith, P.H. (1970), 'Historical Explanation', *Mind, Science, and History, Contemporary Philosophic Thought, the International Philosophy Year Conferences at Brockport*, Vol. 2, SUNY Press, Albany, N.Y., 212—33.

Nowell-Smith, P.H. (1981), 'History as Patterns of Thought and Action', *Substance and Form in History*, University Press, Edinburgh, 145—55.

Popper, K.R. (1936), Lecture on 'The poverty of historicism' attended by Hempel in Brussels; later published in *The open society and its enemies* (1947) and *The poverty of historicism*.

Taggart, F.J. (1942), 'Causation in historical events', *J. hist. ideas*, 3, 3—11.

Trevellyan, G.M. (1938), *The English Revolution*, 1688—9, 105—6

Webb, D.A. (1944), 'The place of mathematics in scientific method', *Hermathena*, 64, 64–87.

White, Morton (1965), *Foundations of historical knowledge*, Harper & Row, New York.

White, Morton (1969), *Foundations of historical knowledge*, Harper & Row, New York.

4 Types of historical explanation within the covering-law model[1]

It is widely though not universally agreed that something like the Popper-Hempel 'covering-law' model is required for *all* historical explanation, which consists of explaining particular events by particular events under the linkage of a generalisation or law (the 'covering-law'). However controversial the issue may be, in this chapter the covering-law model is presupposed: the present aim is to delineate explanation by particulars that fall under the covering-law model (at least according to covering-law model theorists).

In doing this I owe much to the stimulus of Robert Brown's anatomy of questions in his *Explanation in Social Science,* though my version differs noticeably from his in having a much more specific framework or typology. I would also acknowledge the careful work of White (1965) and the masterly elucidations of Murphey (1973). I divide questions of a historical kind into three main types, with a number of subsidiaries. N-type questions are answered by narratives, and are concerned with origins, processes, and circumstances (such questions may be despised by some philosophers of history; I do not regard them as particularly interesting, I urge only that they exist and have a genuine if modest function); the covering laws for such cases are usually trivial. P-type questions are answered in terms of the aims of (mainly) persons, and are concerned with goals, purpose, and design (which some philosophers of history regard as constituting the entire field; but I would urge that such matters constitute only the beginning of historical enquiry).

These two types may be thought of as corresponding to questions concerning the outside of an event or the behaviouristic component of action and to questions concerning the inside (not excluding the outside) of the personal.

In the metascience of the natural sciences, the need for a detailed anatomy of questions hardly arises; but where the social sciences, including history, are concerned it is central, because of lack of specificity in questions in this field as they are usually raised. We may now proceed to lay out a new anatomy. It should be borne in mind, however, that most historical examples in practice are mixtures of these N-type and P-type questions, and even of the sub-types within them. And most philosophers of history regard these two types together as constituting the entire field.

The reason for mapping types of question lies firstly in the widespread propensity to treat one or other of them as the sole exemplar, a tendency that can be shown to be lacking by the simple expedient of distinguishing the rest. Secondly, it displays sharply the field of explanation by particulars, as distinct from general explanation, typical of (natural) scientific theory. And thirdly, if there is the possibility of types of historical explanation beyond those that consist of explanation of particulars by particulars, serviced by covering laws, a clear typology of particular explanation would probably point the way to such further types.

N1: 'What type of origin?'

It will serve several different purposes to provide both physical and social examples of questions. Thus, an insurance assessor examining the scene of a fire wonders whether to attribute the fire to arson or to a carelessly discarded cigarette. He finds, perhaps, tins of petrol or he finds that the fire started in a place that is normally occupied by collections of wood shavings. Again, the question may concern the origin of the moon, and more specifically, whether it originally formed part of the earth. In this case the assessor goes and collects a specimen of dust and rocks from the moon, analysis of which shows that they could not have originated in the earth. These questions are exactly paralleled by one concerning the outbreak of a war, whether it originated in a border incident or in what is relatively speaking an accident, such as the murder of the Austrian Archduke which was the exciting cause of World War I, or whether it stemmed from some dispute or insult. Likewise, the Russian revolution had its origin in the circumstance that the Germans allowed Lenin passage through Germany to Russia. Again, we may wonder about the origin of the different rules of the road and may discover that at one time it was the universal practice to travel on the left because when driving a horse it was natural to sit on the right holding the reins with the left hand behind the right hand, but that Napoleon deliberately altered the rule of the road to confuse his enemies.

These examples may all be characterised as having an explanation consisting of *sufficient datable antecedents*. (It is only for very restricted purposes that such answers suffice; most of them form the start of further questions about the thoughts, intentions, and so on of persons.)

N2: 'In what manner?'

As examples of such a question we may consider the situation where the coastline has certain indentations with trees at the top of cliffs with roots exposed, which we may attribute to coastal erosion. Or, we may notice that groups of mountains are rather like hemispheres, round and not very high, as contrasted with mountains in other parts of the world which are tall and have sharp peaks. The former situation we may attribute to the Juggernaut effect of glaciers. Or, we may wonder about the time lag that ensues between a stimulus that a person receives, say when driving a car, and the slight passage of time that has to elapse before he reacts to it (by putting his foot on the brake). This delay we may attribute to the time it takes for neurones to fire. In a similar way we may be concerned with the question of bitterness characterising the aftermath of a civil war, and this we may attribute to the ruthlessness of internecine strife. Or, we may ask how it came about that France fell in 1940, seeing that she had as large an army as Germany and one that was as well equipped. This we may answer by pointing to the way that France was undermined from within, thus sapping the morale and the communications of the army.

Such questions are concerned less with origin than with the subsequent processes that took place, and the explanations are characterised as consisting of *sufficient antecedent processes*. (Again there often arise further questions about the thoughts, intentions, and so on of persons. Some readers will also note, however, that generalities are embedded.)

N3: 'What web of circumstances?' (or 'What situation?')

An example that may appear to be social because it involves people but is fundamentally to do with physical factors concerns Scott's disaster at the South Pole in 1912. When the small group left their last camp for the Pole, one of them suffered a cut and contracted gangrene, and as a result slowed up the progress of the party. They struck a totally unexpected blizzard which made it impossible to go on. In addition, the party found the tins of cooking oil had leaked. This was in fact due to the unexpectedly low temperatures, -50°C instead of

−40°C. It was at that time not known that the tins would leak at these temperatures. Thus there was a whole concatenation of circumstances that led to the disaster. (I do not mean they are the whole story — there are social and moral factors not included among them — but they can be used on their own to explain a good deal.) Again, if we want to account for the differences between various kinds of monkeys in different places, we may find this explained by mutations plus the fact that in different geographical surroundings the same mutations received quite different kinds of discouragement. Or again, if we are concerned with the explanation of such a strange product in the world as coal, we may attribute it to very complex climatic conditions a very long time ago, consisting of the growth of forests, the absence of destruction of the forests by fire or by rotting, the preservation by burial under a mantle of earth, appropriate pressures and non-violent seepage of liquid with suitable minerals. Again we may consider a different kind of example, such as the Act of Union that took place between England and Ireland in 1800 absorbing Ireland in the United Kingdom. There were strong forces pulling both ways, those who wished to have more centralised power centred in London, those who felt that this would damage Dublin as a capital, those who felt that the change would infringe national sovereignty or perhaps what would nowadays be called national identity, those who felt on the other hand that trade and prosperity would be greatly improved for Ireland, and coupled with all this was the fact that the power to decide lay with a fairly small number of people representing in the main one sectional interest — a fair soil for a mixture of pragmatic and ideological argument eked out with some bribery. Such a web of circumstances had additional importance because it might not have taken very much to alter the scales if a suitable lever could have been found to apply at the right moment.

Again it is worth considering further the example of World War I. The actual situation was not simply retaliation for the murder of the Archduke Franz Ferdinand. The Austrian Government was thirsting for blood, as is evidenced by the fact that although the Serbs conceded everything demanded in the Austrian ultimatum the Austrians still wanted to proceed. Now this in itself would not have been sufficient because there were complications to consider. The Russians were allies of the Serbs and certain to go to their aid. Germany was committed to join Austria if Russia intervened. France was an ally of Russia and had a treaty obligation to support Russia. And finally Great Britain had a similar obligation to go in with France. None of these was secret and the entire situation was well known to all the governments concerned. The actual outcome hinged on whether any of the Powers could, or would, intervene suitably. The most decisive action lay with Germany; for if Germany had intimated to Austria that it would be better to hold off, there would have been no war. Even within Germany the issue was not completely certain in its outcome, for the Cabinet was divided. But here again there was a web of circumstances interrelating the warlords and the peace faction; in the event the militant element, headed by the Kaiser, Wilhelm II, gave the go-ahead to the Austrians. Closely connected with this, however, was another factor. Just as the positive demand for the war came essentially from Germany, so a negative absence of control characterised the British Government, which disabused the German Government too late of the hope that Britain would stay out. (One could, of course, add further features, such as that on the one hand German diplomats of any merit should have known that Britain must and would join in for a number of reasons, while on the other the British disposition towards understatement and not letting their intentions be clearly understood — or rather loudly expressed — coupled with the German inability to see the seriousness behind the British mildness, all contributed significantly to the end result.)

All these examples of complicated warp and weft may be explained as due to *sufficient antecedent interactions*. Leaving aside questions of motive, they are all forms of what may be called the detective hypothesis. (Again, one would often want to go on to further questions about the aims of persons.)

In laying out this anatomy, I am not suggesting that White and Murphey failed to recognise narrative explanations; my purpose is to distinguish them sharply from others and to depict their sub-types.

About these three sorts of questions, N1, N2, and N3, it seems clear that in many cases the answers supply all we want to know and are satisfactory answers to legitimate questions whether of some form of natural science, some form of social science, or of history. Where this is so, the questions can be answered, so to speak, by inspecting a cine-film of the times, eked out by tape-recordings. Such questions might be thought of as seeking videotape answers, supplemented by minimal interpretations of caused connections (cf. White, 1965, Ch. 4). They are concerned roughly with what Collingwood (1946) has called the 'outside' of an event. What they have in common is that they are *narrative* explanations (N for narrative). They are often, perhaps usually, however, insufficient. For example, if we locate the origin of an aeroplane crash in a broken bolt, we may begin to wonder why this should have happened and to entertain the possibility that something serious may underlie this. We are usually not content with explaining the origin of World War I by the murder of the Archduke, we want to understand a great deal more about the circumstances. In other words with an example of this sort we very quickly leave the question N1. Again, if we are considering the manner of the fall of France, while it is essential to understand this in some detail, we very quickly change our focus of interest to the question of what it was that undermined the morale of the country. And in the case of webs of circumstances, e.g. with World War I, seeing that all the relevant features of the political situation were either well known or could quite easily have been understood by all the parties concerned, we may wonder whether there was not some other factor at work that led the main participants to disregard these factors. Thus, it is not that these questions are inadequate or ambiguous or faulty in any way, it is simply that, while they ask all we wish to ask in some cases, in others they are not the full questions that we wish to answer.

The position may be made clearer by referring to Collingwood's view. N-explanations here concern roughly the 'outside' of an event — and Collingwood agreed that explanation can begin with this even if it does not end there. He held, however, that the 'outside' was an abstraction from a total event, informed by an 'inside'. I do not disagree at all.[2] What I do urge — I think Collingwood might have agreed but thought it unimportant — is that 'outsides' can be linked together for humble explanatory purposes. For fundamental explanation, this group is of no interest. I am not concerned to claim their deeper relevance; only to urge that they constitute a genuine, if lowly, type of historical explanation, which can have considerable application in practical matters of everyday life.

Having found their place, I leave them behind for others of a different group.

P1: 'For what target?'

Examples of this kind of question are the following. 'Why did you go into that shop?' Answer: 'To get some tobacco.' This is a complete explanation in some cases. Again, 'What was the Government's object in devaluing the pound?' Answer: 'To restore the balance of payments.' Again, 'How is it that in the last few years magistrates are being pressed not to give prison sentences for first offences, especially of a more or less trivial character?' Answer: 'To relieve pressure on prisons and to avoid bringing young and possibly more or less law-abiding people into contact with old lags.'

In such cases the target can be stated and for some purposes the answer in terms of it may be sufficient.

P2: 'What is the point of a certain target?'

An example would be: 'Tobacco enables me to get through some rather trying work more easily.' Again, the point of controlling the balance of payments is to ensure that a country will be able to continue its import of vital necessities; which would cease to be so if it could not maintain its balance of payments, and if the falling-off of

56

vital imports would lead to inflation and hardship. Again, what is the point of keeping first offenders out of prison? Why not punish them in this way, even if it involves contact with old lags? Answer: 'The point is to decrease recidivism.'

P3: 'What is the (deliberate) systemic design involved?' (or 'What is the policy?')

As an example, the systemic design behind getting through one's work with less irritability would be to promote a more equable frame of mind during the work, afterwards leaving one free of exhaustion and tension. Again, the systemic design behind a number of measures controlling inflation, increasing taxation, especially death duties, supertax, dividend limitation, nationalisation, etc., could be to 'reduce income disparity' or to promote democratisation. Again, the systemic design behind actions aimed at the welfare state, decreasing recidivism and the like, might be to promote a healthier society and to devote its resources towards other ends. Part of the policy (there were other considerations also) of making Eisenhower generalissimo was to preserve harmony. It might be said that if the Allies had had a better generalissimo (in the sense of a better military mind), such as Alanbrooke, Mountbatten, or even Montgomery, the war would have been won a year earlier, but that without the harmony induced by Eisenhower the Allies, so far from winning earlier, would not have won at all.

The terms used in the P-questions were introduced to avoid the ambiguities of those customarily used, e.g. 'purpose', 'end', 'goal', 'reason', 'intention', 'motive', which could be used in any of the three types of questions.

The linkage between the different types of P-answers is that they are all explanations in terms of *persons,* or sets of persons (P for person).

Some such designs may not be deliberately sought; but this will not be discussed just now.

Questions of the P-type cannot be answered with videotape without interpretation over and above interpretation of causal connection; but N-questions, taken strictly, can — they are concerned with an abstraction near to what Collingwood has called the 'outside' of an event. The N- and P-questions have been isolated deliberately from one another, because they can just occur on their own. But in doing history we most commonly find them construed as PN-questions — narratives in which the thoughts, intentions, aims, and so on of persons or groups of persons are included. Thus even the chapter of mechanical accidents in the South Pole example hinges on the mores of not abandoning an injured comrade. And, as Goldstein (1970) has pointed out to me further, a significant factor was the faulty *knowledge* about tins leaking at low temperatures.

That all these types of explanation can be mingled — and usually several of them are — can be illustrated by the outbreak of World War I. The 'origin' lay in the murder of the Archduke Franz Ferdinand; there was a web of circumstances consisting of the treaties between the Powers; the manner in which the culmination came about is to be seen in the haste and absence of negotiation between the opposing Powers; the intention or target of key individuals headed by the Kaiser to support his ally, the point being to enlarge hegemony; and with the systemic design of a policy (conceivably, though this sort of facet is easier to come by in other sorts of excuse) of engaging in a test of manhood without which man becomes decadent.

Many philosophers have restricted historical explanation to P-type answers; virtually all to P-type or to PN-type answers.

Certain reflections will now be appropriate on covering laws.

(a)   The questions of the first group are not so common in the natural sciences as in the social sciences. This reflects not so much a metascientific difference but a difference in man's interests. Thus, the explanation of the formation of coal, while of enormous specialist interest, carries less stimulus for practical purposes than questions about the web of circumstances behind the outbreak of a war, a new piece of legislation, the generation gap, and so on. But it should not be overlooked that these questions do occur in the natural sciences and in their own setting are of vast importance. One has only to reflect on the numerous numbers of questions characteristic of geology, astronomy, economic history, and the evolution of animals and men.

(b)   The second group of questions is unusual in being restricted to matters human. There is no counterpart in the area of the natural sciences. This is simply because they are all questions to do with the deliberate actions of human beings. If there were deliberate actions by atoms or stars we should have a parallel, or if the motion of the stars were brought about animistically, but it is no longer a part of natural science to suppose that this is the case.[3] We shall see, however, that this group is very far from being characteristic of the basic questions in the social sciences.

(c)   All these questions have answers that are characterised by being particular. The explanation may involve more than one particular, but there is no overt reference to anything other than a particular. More explicitly, one objective was to depict the types of explanation of particulars by particulars. Indeed, the anatomy unfolded above could have been entitled 'Types of explanation by particulars', which might have made things clearer for some readers. I wished, however, to conduct the enquiry in the context of history, because historical explanation is commonly equated with explanation by particulars.

Conclusion

It should perhaps be noted that the method of presentation involves little in the way of argument: the procedure has been simply to show the existing specimens; the types arise by filling in gaps left by the commonly accepted types.

In setting forth the anatomy of types of historical questions, several ends have been subserved. One, which though incidental here is of importance in its own right, is to bring out the parallelism between historical questions in natural science and in social science, for the parallelism holds to an extent unrealised by many social scientists. Another is to show the boundaries of what is most commonly regarded as historical enquiry — so that such a limitation on history can be challenged with some precision. The reader will find a stimulating challenge in Munz (1967). But the main objective is to bring out the linkage between commonsense explanation (in the previous chapter), historical explanation, and such part of it as consists of explanation of particulars by *particulars*. The common ground covers a great proportion of the routine 'bolts and nuts' work of sociologists, and, unless it is clearly delineated, the role of generality in the social sciences can become virtually forgotten.

Notes

1 Based on part of a paper given to the Oasis Club, University of Toronto, 23 January 1970. I wish to thank Professor Leon Goldstein for writing me detailed, pertinent, and most helpful comments, which I have drawn on heavily, though he might not agree with my handling of various matters. I have also made considerable use of some valuable comments made by Dr Louis O. Mink.

2 Collingwood's distinction (and the importance of understanding the thought of historical figures and of re-living such thoughts), which I accept, does not necessitate his contentions, which I do not accept, that causation is irrelevant, that to discover what happened is to discover its explanation, and that re-living thoughts is sufficient for doing history — this test is an excellent way of getting brilliant hunches, but they have then to be subjected to historical checking.

3 Up to 1543, however, it was natural, rather more than less, for intellectuals to think of physical motion as divinely instigated (after that rather less than more).

References

Atkinson, R.F. (1972), 'Explanation in History', *Proc. Arist. Soc., 72,* 241–56.

Brown, Robert (1963), *Explanation in Social Science,* Routledge & Kegan Paul, London.

Collingwood, R.G. (1946), *The Idea of History,* Clarendon, Oxford.

Goldstein, Leon (1970), personal communication.

Hempel, C.G. (1959), 'The Function of General Laws in History', *Theories of History,* ed. Gardiner, New York.

Munz, Peter (1967), 'The Skeleton and the Mollusc: reflections on the nature of historical narratives', *The New Zealand Journal of History, 1,* 107–23.

Murphey, M.G. (1973), *Our Knowledge of the Historical Past,* Bobbs-Merrill, Indianapolis.

White, Morton (1965), *Foundations of Historical Knowledge,* Harper & Row, New York.

5 General explanation in history

Whether or not the 'covering-law model' of historical explanation is defensible — and that question is not the subject of enquiry here — its context is the range of historical explanation of particulars by particulars. I will take it we could lay out an anatomy of common historical questions, consisting of two main types — narrative questions (N-questions), about recordable events, and person questions or action questions (P-questions), about the thoughts, aims, and the like of persons — with sub-types of both; moreover, in practical cases some or all of these are likely to be blended together (PN-questions).

The tacit assumption has virtually always been made that historical explanation is restricted to explanation by particulars. But, challenging the assumption, we can raise the question whether narrative and person questions are all that make up history, whether explanation by particulars is the only kind of historical explanation; or, what would be the same thing, whether there are not general laws or theories that have a role in historical explanation very different from, wider and more fundamental than, that of 'covering laws' — which on the covering-law model merely sanction explanation of particulars by particulars. Different parts will be found to be played by these laws, apart from servicing particular explanations.

On non-trivial covering laws

Popper (1963) made it a strong point that covering laws are (nearly always) trivial. (Presumably he was misled by taking 'ordinary' political history as his model. And presumably his motive was to show why laws do not figure in history — political history — books.) Is this so elsewhere? The law that a cigarette burns dry wood shavings may be trivial, but the laws about the formation of coal are not. The law that war follows when an ultimatum is defied may be trivial, but the effect of understatement about foreign policy in relationships between governments is not. The soothing effect of tobacco may be trivial, but the detrimental effect upon recidivism or prison sentences for first offenders was difficult to discover at all and also to establish. The conclusion that the moon was not originally part of the earth hinges on a whole crop of known laws of an advanced nature relating to chemistry and physics. 'Adverbial' explanation as a rule does not appear to be of very great significance on its own account as a distinctive type; but it undoubtedly occurs, and in practice it is most important in some contexts: thus in a medical examination the manner in which a patient moves his finger to his nose may be all-important for purposes of diagnosis. And this takes us into the realm of causal laws in neurology.

Geology uses non-trivial laws from physics and chemistry in dealing with the history of the Earth. Economic history relies heavily on economic laws. Astronomy is parasitic on physics. And possibly some human actions depend on far from trivial psychological laws. In such fields the point is obvious. But it is more striking when found in 'ordinary' (political) history.

It would not be worth opposing the view that the laws involved in history are trivial if that were all — trivial or non-trivial. Quite apart from other social scientists, many historians, in addition to being concerned with the origin, manner, and web of circumstances in explaining what has come about, are also deeply concerned to explain the gaps left by these questions or answers. Thus, Lecky found no answer in the most ordinary historical senses, that is to say none connected with origin, manner, or web of circumstances, to explain the decay of the belief in witchcraft. But when a historian, at least of a certain sort, does think he has a relevant and appropriate generalisation such as one about the 'frontier mentality' to explain much of America's horizontal and vertical mobility and individualism, he does not hesitate to include it as part of the subject matter of the history he is concerned with. Thus Murphey (1973 pp. 83f) has used this example and elsewhere cites the concern with generalisations by the eminent American historian Miller (1939), who utilised it in his *New England Mind*, and Morgan (1956) in his *Puritan Family*. So even the claim is unacceptable that it is not a historian's job *qua* historian to search for and establish laws. A beautiful example concerns a geologist who had to become his own technologist, for there was a gap in current physical and chemical knowledge and his colleagues failed to come to his aid. Thus, in trying to explain coastline patterns and other phenomena, Wegener had to form his own theory of continental drift and even seek to test it. This example epitomises the position even though it is from a natural science; but the examples taken from 'ordinary' history carry the same message. Similar points have been made by Goldstein (1967), as well as by Murphey. Since laws of this type are a focus of interest and therefore challengeable but also provide cover, they may be called the CC-type (challengeable cover).

It is worthy of note that there can be, as it were, an oscillation between a particular explanation and its covering law as the explanatory focus, depending on the problem-situation. Thus White (1969) cites the example from Hart and Honoré (1959) of a man with a stomach ulcer who gets an attack of indigestion after eating parsnips. Is the cause to be located in the parsnips or in the ulcer? A doctor might go either route according to the situation and the problem. White considers that the doctor would focus on the ulcer and the man's wife on the parsnips. But this over-simplies the medical approach: thus if the doctor is concerned with curing the patient, or rendering him able to eat normally, he will regard the ulcer as the cause. But if for some reason the ulcer is not amenable to treatment, the doctor may prescribe a restricted diet that excludes parsnips, and then if they are eaten they are the cause — even from a sophisticated medical point of view. Thus either the particular conjecture or the general law (in this case disposition) may constitute the explanation, according to the problem-situation, that is, the question asked.

An interesting type of example concerns the question: 'From what personality attribute does a certain change stem?' We might attribute the outbreak of World War II to certain deep-seated character traits in Hitler's make-up, namely his megalomania on the one hand and on the other his denigration of those he considered outcasts, in a setting of disturbed Oedipal relations. Parallel is the well-known physical example of the phenomenon of glass actually breaking, which stems from the potential property of glass to be brittle. A more technical example from the natural sciences would be the phenomenon of volcanic eruption caused by the smouldering of constricted explosive materials waiting to be set in motion. Perhaps ordinary physical density affords an even better example: one speaks of the density of a substance such as lead or gold as if it were an entity in nature. One would explain that gold sinks in water because it is so dense. In fact, of course, the assertion of density is the assertion of a generalisation, namely that the weight per unit volume of all gold is 20. In the Hitler example, we would explain his actions by (to condense it) his ideals and his hatreds — which are generalisations like that of the density of gold — perhaps seen against the background of the Oedipus complex.

It should be stressed, as recognised by Hempel (1965), White (1965, pp. 47f), and Murphey (1973, pp. 76f), that although the assertion of a disposition about a particular person, such as Hitler, may appear to be a particular, nonetheless its mode of operation is general, in that a disposition is open-ended in its ramifications.

In these examples of non-trivial covering laws, the explanation of particulars by particulars is not simply parasitic on the laws; the laws are not the sole focus of interest: the particular that explains by means of one of these also remains a focus of interest. Thus the particulars and the laws share our interest. Moreover, and this is more germane, the laws are not *systemic:* the subject-matter they deal with does not involve properties of a system — but this will become clearer, by contrast, after the next type of law has been depicted.

Much broader questions can be found, which are radically different from the types already considered; two closely connected types may be distinguished:

F1 'What institutional systemic need (unrecognised) does a certain entity fulfil?'

Examples under this heading would be these. What underlies imperialistic expansion? One answer might be that it affords an outlet for the youngest sons of the upper classes, or a population outlet. An obvious model on which this might be based could be to ask what need is subserved by the heart, and the answer is that it is to circulate the blood by pumping. A more deep-seated example, in the sense that what underlies it either is not known or is a matter of considerable dispute, would be to ask what is subserved by the incest taboo. Naturally, a low level of answer to this is possible: it is to prevent marriage or sex taking place within the family, where the family may be understood to be the nuclear family or the extended family or the clan, according to the type of society in question. However, if we take the question to mean what is subserved by prohibiting such relations within the family, we make the presumption that the society, at least in its own view, would be somehow adversely affected in a grave way if the taboo were not observed (though what the effects would be are not regarded as capable of being pinpointed by the members of the society). These examples are what are ordinarily referred to as functional explanations. But with the last of them we are moving to the next type of question, moving from institutional need to societal need as a whole.

F2 'For what societal systemic need (unrecognised) is a certain event enacted?'

As an example of this one might mention present-giving. Present-giving is a most interesting phenomenon which may have a variety of meanings in different cultures or even within one culture. Lévi-Strauss (1964) has drawn attention to three uses of present-giving among

64

certain primitives: one is to gain status for oneself, another is to put the recipient under an obligation to return at least as good a present if not a better one, and thus possibly to strain his resources or humiliate him, and the third may be to proffer a token of friendship eschewing mutual aggression. The last one of these may be overtly recognised and possibly the others also.

This question is closely allied to the previous one and may shade into it, in that giving a present to obtain a better present in return may subserve the systemic need for exchange of goods, but the other aspects of it would seem not to be focused on achieving something so much as to constitute an *expression.* In other words, the giver wishes to express his own improved status or superior status to the recipient (it is then of course another question why this expressive need is experienced in society). One more example worth mentioning is the custom of throwing rice at a wedding. This would seem to serve no particular purpose, satisfy no systemic need or social need, but it could be symbolic activity expressing fertility.

It may be noticed that the underlying law here is especially the focus of interest, as compared with the 'covering law' involved in explanation by particulars. For example, F1 virtually answers the question about imperialistic expansion by a generalisation rather than by a particular happening. That is to say, the generalisation is almost immediately the focus of interest, and the same is true of F2. Unlike the questions in N and P, this group is more properly to be answered by saying that the explanations involved are general. So these questions need as a prerequisite a dividing line between particular explanations and general ones. The 'covering law' is the main focus of interest; and it is not trivial, far from it.

Let us now scrutinize the F-questions. What the answers to these two types of questions have in common is that they are both types of *function-explanation* (F for function).

Now it seems to me that this last group of F-questions, which point beyond individual human action and which are *general,* constitute a basic kind of question in the social sciences, whereas the N- and P-questions are concerned with particular explanations only. Significant as these are for practical purposes, the social sciences cannot be restricted to explanations of N- and P-types, and the real metascientific interest begins with F-questions, where we are overtly dealing with generalisations or laws. The foregoing discussion may smack too much of anthropology for the historian. Does history also use F-type explanations?

As regards F1, anthropological as it is, we already have an answer: the history of the British Commonwealth for some historians would inevitably bring in the place of younger sons. F2, equally anthropological, can be illustrated from history. Thus if we ask what led to the abolition of slavery in Great Britain, the answer in trivial historical terms would be simply that the law was altered or that Wilberforce carried out a successful campaign against slavery. But we might be asking for the underlying condition; and the condition required to answer this question would presumably be that public opinion would no longer tolerate the notion of slavery. The societal systemic need would be a growing sense that fellow men should be treated in some measure as human.

If we are dealing with the history of man's lot, we may be more concerned to emphasise the consequences of the abolition of slavery. But if we are dealing with the history of social reform, we shall be specially concerned with the disposition of the country, in developing a new outlook about the place of man. We have therefore to make sure that we have decided which question we wish to answer. In some cases we may simply need to know the historical answer to an enigma in terms of a circumstance that happened, while in other cases our interest may be focused on the underlying state of affairs. In the social sciences questions usually are phrased sufficiently ambiguously that it is not clear which type of question is asked, although the context will often make this clear. Nonetheless, when an overt discussion of such matters is being given, the full distinction should be drawn. Thus in asking a question we should formulate it fully either to bring out what historical circumstance can be located which led up to a certain phenomenon, or to bring out, if we wish to ask the other question, what underlying condition is to be found in history that is to be held accountable for the phenomenon in question.

These questions centre on laws that are of a different type from N- and P-type laws: those, while giving cover to particular explanations, yet being of interest in their own right, did not reveal anything of a systemic character; the present types, function-explanations, are explicitly systemic. And the illustrations should have made the difference clear.

Thus we have two types, apart from sub-types, of laws that have a part to play over and above that of merely servicing particular explanations. But we have not yet reached the end.

Let us now consider the question:

T: 'Do group-phenomena require a dynamic social structure?'

If it is true that the social sciences, including history, presuppose and focus on generalisations and laws, what is the position about abstract theory — that is to say, theories that embody what are sometimes called theoretical entities or unobservables (T for theory-type explanations)? The natural sciences thrive on these and are rich in examples of them. In the social sciences, however, examples are extremely hard to come by, but a few may be mentioned.

The first most obvious example is Marx's socio-economic determinism, which perhaps has not done much to endear the possibility of such theories to many western thinkers. Whether or not the specific form he gave of it is a full-blown scientific theory is still open to dispute, but it is still a candidate for being a theory of the present category and can serve as an example.

Another example comes from Mary Douglas's work (1966) on Jewish taboos. She took as her problem the existence of various kinds of these taboos. She sought to explain them, not, however, in terms of concepts normally accessible to Jews; she sought instead some general feature of Jewish social structure of which they would be most unlikely to be aware). She located this in a virtually philosophical attitude toward *natural kinds*. The niceties of what discriminates one natural kind from another do not concern us here. Let it suffice that there are differences of natural kinds, that is to say, enormous differences, though they might be drawn where other people might think fitting — as for example in regarding milk and meat as different natural kinds. What this leads to is a taboo on mixing natural kinds in certain circumstances.

Such an answer does not of course preclude a further question concerning the origin or explanation of the existence of such an attitude. But so far as it goes this attitude functions as an explanatory factor embedded in the social structure.

Here is another example, all the better for being difficult to classify either as history or sociology or social psychology. It is the question: 'How was it that Butler came to be passed over as Prime Minister of the UK?' and the question is of course all the sharper because he came to be passed over on two separate occasions. (There was indeed a third but he could hardly have been considered a strong runner on that occasion.) Butler was passed over, it will be remembered, first in favour of Macmillan and later in favour of Sir Alex Douglas-Home. No doubt he made some enemies, perhaps because he did not suffer fools gladly and had a somewhat caustic wit, which probably found its way back to its targets, and like anyone he may have made some tactical errors. But these are relatively minor matters and would apply to almost anybody. Now it would seem that Butler suffered from two great drawbacks. He was intellectual, added to that intellectually able, and he had ideas. His intellectual attainment would not matter if it were duly concealed. His opponents apparently had no problem about concealing their intellectuality, and neither of them was burdened with ideas. A step in the explanation to be offered, then, is that England had a disposition of distrust toward politicians who are enterprising in times of peace. To pursue this attitude more deeply, the English are well known to have a deep dispositional distrust of brains. It has traditionally been put that character is more important than brains. That is to say, brains are in some way or other unhealthy, or apt to be a sign of weakness of character.

It will be noticed that, if a historian or social scientist accepted such an explanation, he could well embody it in writing the story of the times as part of the material of history. And yet it is very far removed from the unique particular that is so fondly ascribed to the libido of historians. These examples serve to illustrate something very different which goes beyond what is to be found in generalisations and laws.[2]

General explanations and their place in particular explanations

My springboard, not argued here, is that, although no working historian may invoke the covering-law model, it has to be retained as a presupposition. From this starting point, the chapter is concerned with the possibility that only a certain set of historical explanations is concerned solely with particulars, allowing no interest in their servicing laws. On the other hand, I do not wish to go to the other extreme, to deny the existence of such types of explanation, however uninteresting they may be — I am concerned with *all* types of explanation that can occur, whether they make the heart of a historian beat faster or leave him cold. Indeed, although the map of N- and P-explanations is here subordinate to displaying history as overtly concerned with covering laws, not merely as service laws, but as a goal of historical inquiry, nonetheless I would stress that the map of N- and P-explanations by particulars, though subordinate, is important, because it bears widely on problems of metascience. (Thus the delineation of both the type of explanation by particulars and the types that focus on laws underlines the contention by Popper (1964), and following him by Robert Brown (1963), that parallels between the two fields go extremely far if not all the way.)

The historian who is a purist may not consider it his job qua historian to try to establish, or even find, such CC-type or F-type laws. However, if social scientists do not come up to scratch with something required by a historian, he may have to break his own trade-union barriers or faculty boundaries and investigate the relevant laws for himself. However this may be, some historians in fact do just this.

In developing types of explanation in which the law is of interest, a subject of discovery, or a subject of test for the historian, I have arrived at the following either obviously existing types or possible ones. The CC-type involves laws which, as well as providing cover, are empirical — whether of geology and other historical natural sciences or of political history — but they are about isolated aspects of their subject matter. The F-type involves laws that are systemic; they are perhaps still more interesting. And lastly, the T-type of explanation is theoretical in the sense of a theory that has laws under it. The covering-law model needs to be acknowledged — and put in one corner to make room for CC-type and F-type laws, and possibly for T-type explanatory theories. But even in 'ordinary' history the CC- and F-type laws — and possibly even T-explanations — can form an integral part of the historical story. And in this respect political history is no different from geology, astronomy, or economic history, or evolution.

More explicitly, I wish to stress that F-explanations, or more specifically F-generalisations, may not only be sometimes the main focus of interest of a historical investigation but may also sometimes actually form part of it as quasi-factual material *along with* narrative factors to form an historical explanation (cf. Goldstein 1967, pp. 34—5; Murphey 1973, pp. 84f). And even theoretical structural explanations may do so also. Their position in such cases seems to escape notice by their susceptibility to being condensed into a concept. Thus if we explain that a man sank quickly and was drowned by reason of the bars of gold he had sewn around his waist, we condense a generalisation about gold into the concept of density. This could, of course, be unpacked into the historical event that the man carried so many kilos of gold together with the 'covering law' that 1cc of gold weighs 20 grammes. But it can also be interpreted as a generalisation condensed into a particular. While it makes no allusion to the covering law that high density materials sink, it does make a covert allusion to the density generalisation in referring to the gold bars, by conveying that they are 'heavy', the lay equivalent of the concept of density in hydrostatics. (It should be realised that 'heavy' refers not to total weight, for if the man carried an object of the same weight as the gold bars but occupying a huge volume, he would not sink but float.) Again, take the generalisation that, whenever a dictatorship becomes beset with severe social unrest which it cannot bring under control, it foments trouble with another country by ascribing to it hostile attitudes and actions; this will be condensed by an historian into some such concept as 'scapegoat'.

This seems to me to explain why opponents of the covering-law model find that history seen in terms of the model alone looks very thin. On the other hand, those who feel that laws are no part of the historian's concern at all may very well hold this view through overlooking the disguised way in which laws appear as quasi-empirical material in history.

Thus historians cannot get very far, even though they can get some way, with narrative-explanation and person-explanation *alone,* even in combination. They will have often to include in the person-narrative something that makes these forms of explanation difficult to sustain as exclusive — a condensation of a generalisation or even of a theory, treating it in practice as if it were a particular like any other particular in a narrative. *History thus becomes generality-impregnated narrative.*

It is not suggested that this is the only interpretation of history, superseding existing ones. What is claimed is that along with existing interpretations there also exists what seems to have been overlooked hitherto, a different level of interpretation consisting in generality-impregnated narrative.

Notes

1 From *History and Theory*, Volume XV, 1976, pp. 257–66
2 A somewhat similar view, though differently oriented, has been strikingly presented by Peter Munz (1967).

References

Brown, Robert (1963), *Explanation in Social Science*, Routledge & Kegan Paul, London.

Douglas, Mary (1966), *Purity and Danger*, New York.

Goldstein, Leon (1967), 'Theory in History', *Philosophy of Science, 34, 36*

Hart, H.L. and Honoré, A.M. (1959), *Causation in the Law*, Oxford, 33–4

Hempel, C.G. (1965), 'Aspects of Scientific Explanation', *Aspects of Scientific Explanation and Other Essays*, New York, 342

Lévi-Strauss, Claude (1964), 'Reciprocity, the Essence of Life' in *The Family: Its Structures and Functions*, ed. Rose L. Coser, New York, 36–48

Miller, Perry (1939), *The New England Mind*, New York

Morgan, Edmund (1956), *The Puritan Family*, Boston

Munz, Peter (1967), 'The Skeleton and the Mollusc: Reflections on the Nature of Historical Narratives', *The New Zealand Journal of History, 1*, 107–23.

Murphey, Murray G. (1973), *Our Knowledge of the Historical Past*, Indianapolis, 83ff.

Popper, K.R. (1963), *The Open Society and its Enemies*, New York, II, 264

Popper, K.R. (1964), *The Poverty of Historicism*, London.

White, Morton (1965), *Foundations of Historical Knowledge*, New York, 118.

6 Popper's metascience: theoretical explanation, testability, falsifiability, relations of ideas to facts

Popper makes an initial distinction between theoretical science and technology in a broad unsophisticated way, saying that technology is to enable one to *build* or *do* something while theoretical science is to *explain* something. In this way we can hive off technology, since what he is basically concerned with is the metascience of theoretical science. This is all the more important because great numbers of educated people confuse theoretical science or pure science with its practical applications and technology. Failure to make the distinction prevents man from understanding the nature of theoretical science altogether, including its very special role in scientific discovery and even in applications of science. (See Wisdom, 1987.)

Metascience is simply a convenient term to refer to discussions of scientific theories, scientific ideas, scientific aims — in short discussions about every kind of scientific expression as contrasted with the world itself, i.e. with what science is about.

There are perhaps half a dozen stages in the structure of scientific explanation, some of which come in for little discussion because nothing is known about them. Thus nothing is known about the way in which a new scientific idea is discovered; so in developing scientific procedure one begins at a different rung of the ladder. Perhaps the best place to begin is with the notion of a problem. The commonest idea at large is that science begins by looking around and making huge numbers of observations. Thus the statement can be found that astronomers inspect millions of stars and that physicists observe millions of atoms. It is difficult to understand how such ideas can have survived;

for the organisational difficulty of carrying out such observations would defeat the efforts of several lifetimes — if observation of a single atom or a single star took one minute or five minutes, how long would it take to carry out the observation of a million? That kind of belief, whatever else it is due to, suggests that its supporters have had no contact whatever with the practising scientist. The tradition, however, that great numbers of observations constitute a beginning goes back 450 years and has become built into the popular education of the western world. Popper replaces this myth with the contention that science begins with problems.

The notion of a problem has become overworked, however, because in popular parlance it refers to family frictions, work difficulties, shortage of income, and all the troubles the flesh is heir to. For our purposes it might be convenient to put these things under the heading of difficulties and reserve the concept of a problem for things we do not *understand*. Let us distinguish between things that we cannot cope with or have some difficulty in *coping with* and things that challenge our *understanding*. Certainly there can be an overlap since difficulties in life that we cannot cope with may stem from problems that defeat our understanding. Nonetheless it is with this latter aspect that we are concerned in metascience. How, then, does a problem arise?

Popper's approach to the initial point depends upon a general framework of approach that he adopts towards the world. There has been, for several hundred years, the built-in belief that the human mind is a sort of tabula rasa, patiently waiting to receive impressions falling in upon it from the outside world; or it may be likened to a camera taking observational photographs of what is around. In contrast with this passive conception of the human mind, Popper holds that we always approach the world with a host of expectations. Such expectations include our traditional beliefs, our true beliefs, our false beliefs — in short all our ideas, however bizarre, about the world. We move about our business in the world with these expectations, until we receive a shock in the form of an observation which we make that conflicts with some expectations. The conflict between the observation and the expectation is what constitutes a problem. For example there is a case of a youngster sent out to bring in a piece of peat for the fire. The peat was cut in the shape of bricks the size of house bricks. The youngster, who had never handled these things before, stooped down and steadied himself bracing his leg muscles to lift the heavy weight. He did not say to himself 'this is very heavy and I must lift it accordingly'; he simply acted unthinkingly on this expectation. When he gripped the brick of peat and strained to lift it, he nearly fell over backwards because it was virtually a feather weight. This was his observation and it conflicted with his expectation. His problem was to explain why some material things could be so light and differ from the ordinary objects of experience he was familiar with. For Popper there is no difference between this sort of situation and the way in which a problem arises in natural science. For instance, Newton's gravitational theory led to certain conclusions about the motion of the planets around the sun. These conclusions were borne out beautifully by planet after planet. Then one exception was found; the observation of the motion of the planet Mercury did not conform accurately to the expectations derived from Newtonian theory. Thus there was a clash between observation and theoretical explanation. This clash constituted one of the greatest causes célèbres in the history of human thought. The problem was solved by Einstein. The result is obtained not by adjusting Newton's theory in any way but by inventing a new theory — what is known as the general theory of relativity.

Here we find ourselves already passing from the problem situation in which an observation set the cat among the pigeons by upsetting a well established theory, and going on to the next step which consists of what to do about the problem. The next step is to find a new theory that will at the very least explain the discrepant observation.

We next consider the framework of theoretical explanation. It will have begun to emerge that an explanation consists of a theory which is general or of a hypothesis or set of hypotheses which also are general. A general theory can tell us nothing about the world by itself; it is a kind of open-ended promise of all sorts of explanations. But it is vacuous, so to speak, unless combined with a piece of substantial information about the real world. This is referred to as a set of *initial conditions.* To exemplify from Newtonian theory, we have the general premiss, which is a statement of the general theory itself, and the initial conditions, such as the position of the sun, moon, and Earth at any particular time, and from these two premisses we can deduce logically or mathematically some observation, say about the relative positions of the sun, moon, and Earth tomorrow; and then we can proceed to check this prediction by comparing it with the actual observation at the specific time tomorrow. Indeed it is predicted from Newtonian theory with the appropriate initial conditions that the next total eclipse of the sun visible from England will be on 11 August 1999. This can confidently be counted on to turn up as expected within a second or so. This framework, consisting of a general theory, particular initial conditions, and observational conclusion has become known by the description given for it by Josef Kraft. The 'hypothetico-deductive system' is indeed quite old; it was known to the logicians of the past century, but they did not give it a place of central importance. Popper did not invent it; what he did do was make it the most central feature of scientific explanation and point out very significant properties it possesses. We have noticed above that an ordinary expectation can meet with a rebuff, as when the youngster expected a heavy brick and experienced a light one, or in science when the Newtonian theory predicts a certain planetary motion and is rebuffed by the observation of the planet in a somewhat different motion. In both cases we see that the role of the observation is to refute or falsify the theory or the hypothesis. (See Wisdom, 1987, Chapter 6.)

We shall now turn to the general question of testing. Popper's broad notion of testability is that a theory or hypothesis is not something that is capable of being checked by inspection or by observation or by considering the meanings of terms or by any direct procedure. Testing is some form of checking procedure carried out upon the *consequences* of the theory or hypothesis. It is all-important that testability is in terms of consequences; and this is something quite new in the history of ideas.

The next step is to notice that the obvious line of checking that might occur to anyone does not work: that is to say, checking consequences by obtaining *confirmation* of conclusions derived from a theory or hypothesis does not constitute evidence at all. This negative contention of Popper's was also revolutionary. The belief that confirmation of conclusions could be obtained did exist even in the last century; but according to Popper such a procedure is exactly equivalent to the traditional method of induction. Against induction Popper carried out a sustained polemic. Before Popper it had become recognised that inductive inference, so-called, was full of holes. Attempts to plug them had been going on for well over 100 years without result, though it could have been seen that no positive result was possible — in fact this was foreseen 200 years ago by Hume. There are a great many severe criticisms that can be made against induction, but the short way of going about it is to point out that from particular premises, no matter how many of them, no universal or general conclusion follows (even with probability). Otherwise put, it is that an inference from particular premises to a general conclusion is invalid, a point that was well known from the time of Aristotle. Now confirmatory observations of a general hypothesis occupy a position like the premises of an inductive inference, the only difference being that they are conclusions instead of premises. (See Wisdom, 1987, Chapter 6.)

To give an example that will serve perhaps roughly to show why confirmation does nothing to support the general conclusion, consider the following example. Let us form the hypothesis that dramamine prevents sea-sickness. To test this, we set up the required initial conditions, which consist of giving people who are prone to sea-sickness a dose of the drug, and we take them out in a boat on Lake Ontario for the day. It so happens that the day is pleasant and calm and the subjects return home feeling well, so the predicted conclusion that they would not suffer from sea-sickness after taking drugs has been confirmed. But of course anyone can see that this is no support at all.

The subjects could have gone on the lake without any drug at all and would have returned quite well. And the reason for this is important: it is that the day was calm. In other words the initial conditions, that is the state of the day and of the water, provided no test.

We are now in a position to assess what it is that constitutes a test in this case. It would be that the water should be somewhat rough; that is to say, the conditions would have to be such as to give the hypothesis some chance of failing. Popper expresses this in the form that the aim of an experiment is to refute or falsify the hypothesis. Less dramatically put, it is that the experiment is set up so as to make it possible to refute or falsify the hypothesis, *provided* in fact it should be the case that the hypothesis is false. What we then require of a good hypothesis is that it should *survive* falsification or refutation.

Thus testability for Popper comes to be refutability or falsifiability.

The untestable hypothesis is not falisfiable but only confirmable, and, cannot be tested. Indeed he goes further and holds that such a theory or hypothesis is not a scientific one. Thus to be scientific a general statement must be falsifiable or refutable.

This is the most central novelty in Popper's metascience and the one that has created the greatest opposition.

It would be well to underline the salient features of this whole account of metascience. It involves opposition to the notion that knowledge is built up upon observations, and along with that is opposition to the method of induction, which in fact is the classical attempt to build up knowledge upon particular observations. This criticism of the classical approach runs counter to the intuitive notions of metascience that most scientists themselves have. They may not actually work inductively, and indeed if Popper is right they could not work in this way, but they think they do. All down the centuries they have paid tribute to the method of induction and certainly most of them believed they were following it. Most of the great physicists, that is; Darwin was an exception — one would think from some of Darwin's remarks that he had read Popper and read him very carefully. This passive view of observation has been with us for 450 years or more, since the time of Bacon, and has become built in to the intuitive and unthinking approach that scientists and educated laymen have about metascience. They take for granted that science is built upon an observation and that this is what gives it a firm basis. It sounds much less secure to say with Popper that science begins with hypothesis. The traditional view of observation was a simple one: that of being the source and foundation stone of all our knowledge. In Popper, however, observation has two different roles: the first one is to set up a conflict with expectations and hypotheses, making a dent in the corpus of our knowledge by refuting some hypothesis or other and thus giving rise to a problem. The second role of observations is to test the consequence of the hypothesis. It may be noticed that, in this framework, knowledge that is certain can never be achieved, will never build up confirmations. All we ever achieve is refutations that do not come off; that is, we achieve hypotheses that survive falsification tests. When falsification is survived Popper describes the hypothesis as corroborated; but this technical expression used instead of confirmation has a rather bare meaning: it means *only* that a hypothesis has not been falsified. He does, however, go on to a more sophisticated development to do with degrees of corroboration based on the notion of degrees of falsifiability of theories; but an examination of these notions would be required only for a very detailed treatment of Popper's metascience.

There is a verbal feature of great importance which might be easy to overlook. Since it emerges that all our knowledge is tentative or fallible, we soon notice that this not only applies to the general hypothesis but also to particular observations. It is not only general theories that are challengeable and open to refutation; observations are also challengeable and modifiable and even rejectable, although it may only be seldom, nonetheless sometimes they do have to be challenged and are found to be false. How can a carefully carried out observation be false? Popper's answer is that there is no such thing as an observation pure and simple, in the sense of a recording of what is there in front of us in nature. It is not as if observation is the work of a camera which flicks and registers on the sensitive plate a record of what is there. The reason is that observations are recorded by means of concepts, however lowly or humdrum, and all our concepts involve some level, however lowly or humdrum, of theoretical ideas. Thus, to say that one mountain is slightly higher than another one is to say that there is some common base in relation to which both can be measured, and the base is quite a sophisticated notion of sea-level — sophisticated because it is not as if the sea has a permanent level, it is always rising or falling, and sea-level is a very conceptual device deliberately introduced by man. It is in this sort of way that conceptual elements creep into statements of observation and this situation has come to be described in the form that *observations are theory-laden.*

Such a view naturally makes it look as if science is built up on quicksand; for if observations are theory-laden and theories are fallible, then there is no certainty anywhere. But this after all accords with what we must begin to recognise as being the truth about human knowledge and something we must adjust to and live with. The intellectual approach to be sustained is that it is possible to regard knowledge as fallible, yet also possible to use such fallible knowledge with *some* reliability. Considering that for thousands of years man has regarded himself as a fallible creature, it is surprising that people take so unkindly to this sort of metascience. Presumably they had pinned hopes on science for achieving certainty, partly because science is so often mathematical, and mathematics, at least for a very long time, appeared to provide absolutely certain conclusions. However, on Popper's view we have to be content with tentative, fallible explanation, but we have at least that.

A further distinction should be drawn in the explanatory schema. Generalisations constitute the beginning of scientific work (i.e. of course generalisations that metascientists used to think were attained by induction), even though not of scientific thinking. Generalisations means generalisations of observations. Thus 'all gases expand when heated' is a generalisation. By contrast, explanatory theories or groups of hypotheses are not generalisations from experience, and ipso facto they involve concepts that go beyond experience, concepts that are different in kind from those occurring in generalisations. The main feature of explanatory theories or sets of hypotheses is that from them generalisations can be deduced. When this is so, the general theory or set of hypotheses can be said to explain the generalisations. So one of the central operations of science, a key feature of the progress of science, consists in explaining all the generalisations that have been found in the elementary stages prior to finding an explanatory theory. This aim in the case of physics has been very well satisfied. For huge numbers of generalisations explanatory theories have been produced. For example, the great generalisations about planetary motion which were discovered by Kepler at the end of the 16th century were unintelligible before Newton produced his great gravitational theory, which explains them. Newton's theory tells us that the force of attraction between two lumps of matter is obtained by multiplying the masses of the two lumps of matter together and dividing by the square of the distance between them. This is a very simple sort of theory and is more or less intelligible as it stands. Newton's great mathematical achievement was to devise a form of mathematics by which he could deduce from this theory the elliptic motion of the planets and the other laws of Kepler's.

Here we have a distinction between theory and generalisation to each of which fact or observation is differently related; and for an understanding of metascience it is essential to keep this threefold application clearly in mind. For observations can be seen as *instances* of generalisations, whereas they can only be deductive conclusions from *explanatory* theories.

7 Theoretical, applied and technological social science

The main reason for drawing the distinctions under this heading is that they are so often overlooked, even by those in the best position to make them. The broad distinction between theoretical and applied science has long ago been drawn by Popper in the form that the aim of theoretical science was to explain, that is to give an answer to a problem, while the aim of applied science is to do something. Thus, the aim of electromagnetic theory is to explain the complicated general relationships that hold about electric currents and also the relationships between electricity and magnetism, while the applications of this enabled us to make dynamos, run trains, and construct electric heaters as well of course as more complicated modern devices.

There are two purposes to be served by going into this matter more fully. One is that further distinctions have to be drawn. In other words, Popper's designation of applied science does not go quite far enough; but the main concern of importance is that the broad distinction itself is widely overlooked in the field of the social sciences by large numbers of its practitioners but apparently also at times by Popper himself.

To begin with the first of these two considerations, what is needed is a distinction between applied science and technology — made quite generally for all science whether natural or social. The distinction was, I think, first drawn by Agassi (1966). I will first depict it as I see it.

The term 'applied science' is possibly slightly unfortunate and not fully appropriate, but will probably continue to have to serve as a shorthand. It is short for applications of science. The reason it is not quite appropriate is the overtone that there is a second kind of science after theoretical science which is of a different kind. In fact what is involved is simply *using* theoretical science, thus applying it to something or other, but the science is one and the same. For example, Newtonian dynamics is a theory about force. More specifically, it is a theory about the relationship between forces and the accelerations they produce in bodies or in the masses of such bodies. Such a theory is entirely general and independent of any particular application. However, it can be fairly readily and immediately applied to bodies that move in a certain medium. We could, of course, apply it to meteors moving about the atmosphere in a vacuum. This would be the immediate application of the theory in its own terms. But if we apply the theory to bodies moving in air, then we shall be considering questions to do with the fall of an apple, with the flight of a cricket ball, or with the curves described by a shell fired from a gun. Again, we might apply the theory to the motion of bodies in water and this would yield what is known as hydrodynamics.

From these examples it is clear that the applications of a theoretical science can themselves be highly abstract, and conceivably of little or no use for practical purposes. They remain highly theoretical in the sense that they can be used to explain motion in certain conditions and such applications may indeed constitute knowledge simply for its intrinsic interest almost as clearly as the original theory itself.

The application of a theory need not, however, be so rarified and useless as these examples would suggest; for the application of Archimedes' principle of floating bodies can be put to work immediately for the understanding of boats so as not to capsize.

It is when we take an additional step that we enter the field of technology as contrasted with applied science. For instance, let us deliberately think out and utilise the conception of a keel for a boat which sticks out a considerable depth below the boat and which is also fairly heavy in comparison, say, with the wood out of which the boat is constructed; it is then that we have introduced a piece of technology. Thus Popper's notion that *doing* marks a contrast with theoretical science serves appropriately to characterise technology rather than applied science.

It would now be in place to consider the contribution made by Agassi to the distinctions being considered. He was, I believe, the first to draw a sharp distinction between applied science and technology and also to characterise the two fields. Broadly speaking, he considers applied science to be nearer to pure, theoretical science than it is to technology.

Agassi stresses the venturesomeness of doing science and the imaginativeness or inventiveness required to do it. He expresses this very neatly by saying that science cannot be done by means of *algorithms*, that is to say, there is no formula by which scientific discoveries or achievements can be arrived at. On the other hand, he holds that by contrast *technology is algorithmic.*

Agassi also draws a further distinction. The role of success is quite different in science and in technology. While it is true that prediction — successful prediction — occurs in science, this is not one of its fundamental characteristics or even one of its most important features. In technology, on the other hand, successful prediction is paramount. Thus whether or not we can successfully predict the next eclipse of the sun is of minor importance to science; but it is of the utmost importance that the complicated technological arrangements made for landing a manned capsule on the moon should work. Pure science must of course be successful in its function of explaining and giving the answers to theoretical problems, that is, it must be successful in doing its own job. But this is quite different from the success demanded of technology, where failure is unacceptable. If a physicist puts forward a new theory and it does not succeed in explaining a discrepancy satisfactorily, he quite rightly does *not* lose his job. Einstein spent thirty-five years of his life trying to invent his third theory of relativity and was not particularly successful, but no one would have suggested that he should have been dismissed from his post at the Institute for Advanced Studies. On the other hand, if the Concorde super-aeroplane is a failure, probably many careers will reach an untimely end.

It seems to me that Agassi's broad distinction holds. I have used the example of applying Newtonian mechanics to a resisting medium. Another example would be applying Newtonian statics to finding the equation of the catenary, that is to say, of a heavy flexible string hanging in a loop between two nails, or finding densities or melting points. Any of these results might be applied in turn to advancing technology, but without being thus applied they constitute in themselves an application of science which extends our knowledge. Thus applied science is nearer to theoretical or pure science, which is explanatory, in that its function is to promote explanation or understanding, while on the other hand technology has as its function *to do* something.

(It is perhaps important to indicate another distinction. Technology, or rather practical applications, are to be distinguished from *praxis.* Praxis is a post-Marxist doctrine meaning roughly that all genuine theoretical work must result in social applications. Clearly some western science does not.)

It seems to me of vital importance to preserve and emphasise these distinctions. In this scientific age when every magazine refers to science and one would suppose the world's population would take an interest in science and its nature, it is surprising and indeed appalling to find that great numbers of people have very little idea of what science is, and further, that they are not particularly interested in the matter. The appropriate distinctions lead, for instance, to the following consequence. Those who regard science as a sinister thing are clearly not aware of science as theoretical explanation at all: what they are thinking about is technology, not of course the kind of technology that whisks them quickly to a holiday resort or provides them with television, but the kind of technology that threatens to blow them up or to poison the atmosphere they breathe or damage the crops they eat. It is highly desirable that opposition to dangerous technology should be focused where it belongs while the greatness and inventiveness of theoretical science should be salvaged as one of the glories of mankind's creations.

So far, what has been discussed are the distinctions to be made in the field of science and technology in general. The particular kind of science involved was not mentioned and the overall discussion might well have suggested that natural science was the main focus. What is needed now is to consider the matter specifically in relation to the social sciences.

In this area it is somewhat curious that Popper, alive as he was to the difference between science and technology, tended to gloss over the difference in the field of the social sciences. He could not but have been aware of the difference and indeed at times he makes it clear that there is a difference, but at other times he glosses over it. The reason for this probably lies in the fact that he was greatly concerned in his philosophy of the social sciences to oppose totalitarian types of philosophy, and to concentrate on piecemeal changes in society rather than on making drastic changes in society as a whole. Such an aim may well have led him to stress the importance of *doing* in connection with social technology. However, there is no reason whatever to restrict theoretical social science to the totalitarian kinds. On the contrary, it may well be that progress in the social sciences may become possible, as has so often happened in the field of natural sciences, only by making imaginative and highly abstract societal theories. The possibility alone makes it desirable to keep the distinction sharply in mind.

It is very widespread among intellectuals and among social scientists themselves also to complain that there is very little progress in the social sciences and to complain about the absence of laws and theories; and indeed there is much substance in this. The result is that what goes on in these areas consists broadly speaking of two sorts of enquiry. One concerns establishing a great deal of detailed information about a social matter, such as for example depicting what goes on in the day-to-day life of prisons in a certain province. Such investigations are not very like what goes on in the natural sciences and more closely resemble what a high-level civil servant might conduct for a government report. We do not find physicists compiling a report on the detailed information about the constitution of the air at the North Pole. If such information were required, it would be obtained by geographical technologists with a training in physics, but not by physicists. The other activity that engages social scientists concerns theory-construction and frameworks and these topics constitute most of the work done of a theoretical kind, but it does not constitute theory formation. It discusses theory construction but does not construct theories. It seems possible that if social scientists were more alive to the theoretical distinctions drawn between theoretical science and applied science and technology, and that if these distinctions are applied to the field of the social sciences then social scientists would be in a better position to approach their own field of the social sciences with their questions more clearly distinguished. They would have a clear idea of whether they were going to concentrate upon laws or theories, or information gathering, or technology — or even metascience.

To encapsulate:

A theory is exemplified by a theory of motion.

Applied science is exemplified by using this, with certain additional laws, to ascertain that the stars are moving away from us at greater and greater speed. Such applications are highly theoretical.

A technological application would be the surgical use of laser beams on cataracts.

References

Agassi, Joseph (1966), 'The Confusion between science and technology in the standard philosophies of science', *Technology & culture*, 7, 348—70.

Brown, Robert (1963), *Explanation in social science*, Routledge & Kegan Paul, London.

Simon, H.A. (1957), 'Mechanisms involved in pressures toward uniformity in groups. Mechanisms involved in group pressures on deviate-members'. *Models of man*, Chaps 7 & 8 with Guetzkow, H., New York.

Wisdom, J.O. (1964), 'Review of Brown (1963)', *Economica*, 31, 219—20.

8 Are there theories in the social sciences?

What is this question?

It is here assumed that there are social science generalisations, whether universal or statistical. It is further assumed that in the natural sciences the explanatory theories have as their main function the *explanation of generalisations.* (They may also explain particular events. It is clear from examples that such explanation occurs, e.g. the explanation of a solar eclipse by the theory of gravitation. Moreover, generalisations can be used to explain particular events, as a low-level form of explanation; so, if explanatory theories explain generalisations, and generalisations explain particular events, it follows that explanatory theories can explain particular events.) Now explanatory theories may be recognised, of course, by their position in the hierarchy — by their position 'above' generalisations, i.e. they are recognisable by the fact that they explain generalisations. However, theoretical explanations in natural science seem always to possess the interesting and strange characteristic of having at least one term that is 'non-instantiative', what are most often called 'theoretical terms'. (See Wisdom 1972, 1987.)

The question then is: are there theories that explain social science generalisations? And, if so, do such theories contain non-instantiative concepts?

If we exclude economics, as I am doing, as being unlike the typical social sciences, the difficulty of finding examples is enormous. I have searched; in particular I have kept an eye out for them constantly when reading books of various levels of sophistication about the nature of the social sciences. When reviewing Robert Brown's (1963, p. 187) valuable *Explanation in Social Science,* I found in it apparently three examples. A brief examination showed that two did not qualify; but I thought at the time that the third one did. When I had leisure to look up the original, however, it became clear that that example did not qualify either. (See Appendix 1.) (Brown (1963, Ch. XI) *seems* to have operated on the tacit *assumption* that explanation in the social sciences could not have non-instantiative terms.)

Furthermore, situational individualism, which marks Popper's philosophy of the social sciences, and is also held enormously widely in the Anglo-American field of academia, renders it virtually impossible to have non-instantiative concepts. The doctrine means that all social activity can be regarded as the outcome of the aims and actions of individuals confronted with a situation. Hence the basic units are human beings, an instantiative idea; it would not be wholly impossible to combine individuals with non-instantiative ideas, but any attempt to carry this out might tend to be Platonic or Marxian, and would run counter to the spirit of individualism.

Indeed the only sources of non-instantiative concepts, and of theoretical explanations at all, lie in two places which, until recently, were hardly regarded in academic circles as having a serious claim to be possible contributions to knowledge, or even as having a serious claim to be studied at all (if they were both agreed to be myth-making, even their admittedly large *influence* on mankind was disregarded) — Marx and Freud. Yet Marx's theory of the overthrow of capital, even if false, would seem to be a type of explanatory theory with a non-instantiative concept. There could be some dispute about this, because it might be interpreted not as a scientific theory with empirical content but as a form of deterministic metaphysics. But there seems to be little if any doubt that some of Freud's theories, again even if false, qualify. Thus the theory of ambivalence is one (loving and hating the same person at the same time). And, more familiar, the theory of the Oedipus Complex.[1]

Is there a reservation to be made about these? There could be, on the grounds of their being *untestable.* It has been a common charge that they *are* untestable. If there is nothing more to be said here, then they are not *scientific* theories, and so cannot qualify.

They are *untested.*

But *untestable*? What about the transition from being *untested* to being *untestable* (or for that matter *testable*)? For some reason the passage has been glossed over without careful scrutiny. Even Popper, knowing the difference, failed to make it sufficiently explicit. In one paper, however, I (Wisdom 1963) drew attention to the following example. Two of the three classical tests of Einstein's general theory of relativity depend upon observations that can only be made during a total eclipse of the sun. But the Earth might have had no moon. So these two tests depend upon the *accident* of the Earth's having a moon. The third test hinges on the motion of Mercury. But there might have been no such planet, or Mercury might not have been near the sun. So the third test, too, depends on an accident. Indeed, no one might have had the sheer mathematical or the prodigious imaginative ability to think of these tests at all. Then the general theory would have been *untested.* But *untestable*? It would have been untestable *so far as anyone knew,* so far as *our knowledge went*; but it would not have been *untestable in principle.* Popper himself subsequently, in discussion at a meeting, subscribed to the same example to draw the same distinction, i.e. distinguished thereby between untestable and untested.

How is it possible to show that a theory is *untestable in principle*? Logical positivists have long aimed at such an achievement. But it is virtually impossible. It may be that a theory can be shown to be couched in such a form as to preclude testing, say through some subtleties covering up lack of specificity in the theory. I would not claim that this is impossible. I would suggest, however, that caution is needed before dismissing a theory as untestable in principle. (With regard to the testability of some of Freud's theories, I (Wisdom, 1966, 1967) have made a concrete proposal by which they could apparently be tested.)

The easiest and best way to show that there are explanatory theories is to produce one example, even if only one, for one suffices. Until we have one, what is the position? The possibilities are few.

One is that there might be no explanatory theories from which social science generalisations could be deduced. We should have to get along as well as we could with generalisations, which would for ever remain unintelligible in themselves and in their interconnections. Many, perhaps the majority of social scientists, would settle for this. It is probable that the human tendency to try to understand would oscillate between situational individualism, taken to be a framework in which we could rest satisfied with a web of generalisations, and 'psychologism', or psychological individualism, in which social generalisations would be seen as stemming from human nature. When situational individualism began to seem too thin, we should veer over towards psychologism, as when a social anthropologist interprets a ritual symbolically instead of finding out what its practitioners conceive themselves to be doing; and when this seemed dangerously near to being arbitrary and untestable, we might return to situational individualism, as with present-giving when we could find no way of choosing between different psychological interpretations.

But the overall issue is obscure unless we first go on to consider whether non-instantiative terms are likely to have a place or not. Brown (1963, Ch. XI) seems to have *assumed* they have not and to have overlooked their enormous role in natural science theories. And this attitude may seem reasonable enough, because social science explanations would have to be, we may feel, *humanly* understandable, which non-instantiative terms, we may think, would make impossible. This point has been widely expressed in the form that what is relevant to the social sciences is not 'erklären' but 'verstehen'.

Let us first assume such a point of view, that there should not/cannot be non-instantiative terms in social science explanations. We might still go further than settle for a host of generalisations; for it might be possible to assemble some or all of them into a wider generalisation involving only instantiative terms. An elementary example, which I (Wisdom, 1952, pp. 23–5) have drawn from physics, will show what is meant. One gas law is that the volume, v, of a given mass of gas is proportional to the absolute temperature, T, provided the pressure, p, is kept constant. Another is that p is proportional to T, provided v is constant. Now these two laws can be unified, allowing p and v to vary, by the single more complex law that the product, pv, is proportional to T. And this law will do all the work of the other two. Here, granting that the two initial laws are instantiative, so is the more complex combination.

A social science example would be the Homans-Simon theory of group-conformity. Such a consummation, almost never articulated, would seem to be the ideal in the minds of many social scientists. A grand generalisation, yielding all others as particular cases applicable in special conditions, would be highly explanatory and a great achievement.

Two questions suggest themselves. Would anything be missing which we should like to see included in our scientific account of society? And why do we not have wider and wider generalisations building up to a grand generalisation in natural science?

In the beginning to answer these, I would concede that we might well be satisfied with a grand generalisation. Such a concession would not amount to much, however, if it were impossible to achieve such a goal. And — the second of the above questions — this is precisely why we find nothing approaching it in natural science. In natural science we have laws about magnetic attraction and laws about electric circuits, for example, or laws about planetary motion and laws about the motion of comets. But there is no specifiable way we can find a larger generalisation to encompass magnetic attraction and electric circuits, or to encompass planetary motions and comets. Strangely enough, easier than the task of finding such larger generalisations is the extraordinary procedure to be found in natural science of inventing an explanatory theory with non-instantiative terms, such as Maxwell's theory (electro-magnetic equations) and Newton's gravitational theory. The curious outcome of such theories is that they yield the larger generalisations that we are unable to find otherwise. Therein lie the power and beauty of theoretical explanation with non-intantiative terms. Moreover, we can see that they could not yield such generalisations, containing, as they must, a mixture of instantiative terms unrelated in our experience with purely instantiative means; for if they could, this would be equivalent to our finding the larger generalisations directly in the way we find any smaller generalisations. Moreover, Maxwell's equations led to the discovery, not known as a generalisation, that light is electro-magnetic.

Returning now to the social sciences, is it likely that there could be a grand generalisation, obtainable (if we are supremely clever and lucky) without explanatory theories involving non-instantiative terms? The possibility would depend on having something in common between the smaller generalisations which we wish to link. What examples might we be in trouble over?

> The number of suicides varies inversely as the degree of social cohesion (Durkheim)
>
> Groups when frustrated by their leader take refuge in fight or flight (Bion)
>
> Exogamy has the societal function of protecting totemism (or its replacements) (Freud)
>
> Capitalism presupposes the Protestant ethic (Weber)

Can we hope, by generalisation searching, to find a generalisation linking such as these? From the practical point of view of trying to find linkages, it would seem sensible to follow the only course known to the history of human thought, occurring on a fair number of occasions in the natural sciences, of seeking in the social sciences explanatory theories embodying non-instantiative terms.

Appendix 8.1: Professor Robert Brown's *Explanation in Social Science*

This work appeared in 1963. I (Wisdom, 1964) reviewed it appreciatively and I begin by quoting (with purely verbal alteration) the first half of the review, which holds equally well today.

> This is an outstanding textbook in the metascience of the social sciences, a field where such a work is desperately needed. It will not only teach students but also their teachers, for its contents are by no means common knowledge. The author has many appropriate qualities, easy familiarity with several social sciences,

sound metascientific knowledge and skill in the field of the natural sciences, detachment, and balance of judgment. As a result the book is enjoyable to read, so that one is able to forget the poor print and paper (the binding is nice) which comes as a surprise from a major publisher.

In Part I Mr Brown disentangles a number of different kinds of questions that all begin with 'Why?' and he divides social explanation into seven main types. Each of these is given a chapter in the remaining part of the book. An important distinction is drawn between two forms of function-explanation, but the most important discussions concern empirical generalisations and theories, i.e. higher level explanatory theories in the sense understood in the metascience of the natural sciences. Mr Brown is able to show that such theories really do occur in the social sciences. The aim of the work is to disentangle various kinds of explanation in this field, put a host of metascientific questions in the field into proper perspective, show that numerous accusations against the social sciences lack validity (he does this by argument centring on good examples, not by falling back on the defensive), and to bring out the same anatomy and physiology in this field as in the natural sciences.

Apart from the skill with which all this sorting out is done, the most attractive feature of the treatment of the subject is the large number of apt citations from the social sciences that the author includes and makes use of.

The only additional point I might have added at the time is that for his contentions he relied heavily on Popper's *The Poverty of Historicism;* the great value of Brown's detailed work lay in making Popper's available in a readable and simplified form.

The only criticism I would now add is that the typology and explanation is presented as if all types were on the same level; whereas I would consider that historical explanation and generalisations, for example, play very different roles and need to be contrasted instead of being depicted as members of a family.

The review continued:

Here an interesting observation may be made. The author is to be congratulated on unearthing some examples of rarities (e.g. explanatory theories) in the 'social' social sciences, but the greater proportion of his examples are taken from economics. Thus only three out of eight of the examples of well-formed hypotheses are non-economic. Hence, while Mr Brown has established his contentions about the existence and operation of certain things (e.g. explanatory theories) in the 'social' social sciences, the result is nonetheless thin. Better crumbs than no bread, but let us not mistake crumbs for bread.

Alas, on checking up on Brown's three examples, they are found wanting — they lack non-instantiative concepts.[2] Thus one of the theories had to do with probability distributions of changes in attitude. Calculations, or mathematical functions generally, do not render a term non-instantiative. For instance, the average man may have a weight of 70 kg, but if there is nowhere anyone at all of this weight, although there is no instance the term 'average weight' is instantiative, for it could denote an instance.

The best candidate cited by Brown is Simon's (1957) theory of a group mechanism for inducing social conformity, including dealing with deviant members (it is a formalisation of a theory of Homans). Moreover, a new generalisation was obtained about the conditions in which the group disintegrates. The terms involved are the amount of activity imposed on the group by the environment, the level of friendliness, the amount of activity carried on by members of the group, and intensity of interaction; but none of these is non-instantiative.

I would conclude that Professor Brown's dissection of historical and universal generalisations is accurate, but that his account of explanatory theory is seriously inadequate, in failing to take account of non-instantiative concepts.

Appendix 8.2: Friedman on Assumptions

In 1953 Friedman published a most interesting essay on the meta-science of economics (Friedman, 1953). He called it the methodology of 'positive' economics; and by 'positive' economics I think he meant the *empirical content of theories*, i.e. theories about the *functioning of the economy*. Friedman held that the only relevant test of a hypothesis lay in comparing its predictions (or retrodictions) with experience: like Popper he held that if a prediction does not square with a hypothesis, the hypothesis is to be rejected (is falsified as Popper would put it); that survival of a great many opportunities for rejection by predictions gives great confidence in the hypothesis (corroboration in Popper's view) — that we can never 'prove' a hypothesis, only 'disprove' it, or 'fail to disprove' it. (Pure Popper,[3] though Popper is not mentioned.) Further, Friedman held, as regards the checking of predictions, 'Evidence cast up by experience is abundant and frequently as conclusive as that from contrived experiments . . .' (Friedman, 1953, p. 10).

Friedman next went into two ways facts are related to hypotheses.

The second concerns, of course, testing them by their predictions. The first concerns the way facts may enter into the construction of a hypothesis (which facts could indeed include the other facts used for testing). The notion of facts entering into the construction of a hypothesis has an inductive ring about it, suggesting that a hypothesis may be an inductive generalisation from observed facts (Friedman 1953, pp. 13f). Friedman can, however, be freed from such an imputation, simply by replacing the supposed inductive process by one in which the observed facts are characterised as phenomena to be explained, in relation to which the hypothesis is *conjectured* as a possible generalisation explaining them.

Friedman next entered a caveat. Because it can be difficult to find new evidence for an explanatory hypothesis, i.e. finding new consequences of it, there is a temptation to suppose that explanatory hypotheses can be checked, as well as by consequences, by a more direct process. Such a process amounts to the idea that hypotheses contain *assumptions*, the conformity of which to reality can be investigated (independently of their consequences). He held that this idea was wrong and damaging. 'For truly important and significant hypotheses will be found to have 'assumptions' that are wildly inaccurate descriptive representations of reality, and, in general, the more significant the theory, the more unrealistic the assumptions . . .' (Friedman 1953, p. 14) Indeed, 'to be important, a hypothesis must be descriptively false in its assumptions'. The question is not whether the assumptions are descriptively realistic, 'for they never are, but whether they are sufficiently good approximations . . .' (Friedman 1953, pp. 14, 15). And, he continued, the question is answered only by testing the theory, i.e. by its predictions. Hence the direct investigation of assumptions hinges on the fundamental testing of consequences, by observational predictions. (Friedman illustrated from the theory of monopolistic and imperfect competition.)

On the basic question whether a hypothesis can be tested by the realism of its assumptions, Friedman (1953, pp. 16–23) makes a number of important points. Perhaps the chief one is that the 'assumptions' (better 'presuppositions') 'specify the circumstances under which the formula works'. Thus Galileo's formula for a falling body presumes that the bodies fall in a vacuum. Similarly Friedman gives other nice examples, one artificially constructed to do with leaves round a tree showing the unreality of the presuppositions, another to do with shots made by an expert billiard player made *as if* he had *calculated* them, which leads into his excellent economic example about firms behaving *as if* they *calculate* to maximise their profits.

Now the presuppositions may in some cases be *close approximations.* Here Friedman is at pains to point out that there are no definite criteria to tell us how close a 'close' approximation must be. But we do recognise as a rule when it is close enough. This enables Friedman to give an alternative formulation of laws: thus instead of stating a presupposition explicitly, such as being restricted to a vacuum, he can say, omitting the presupposition, that the law of falling bodies holds in a variety of circumstances to a sufficiently close approximation. Nonetheless the explicit presupposition has the advantage of specifying the circumstances in which a theory actually holds.

But in other cases, where the presuppositions are not approximations, they can only be *unrealistic* — that is, in the sense that they do not denote anything accurately or approximately.

About such cases, the broad idea does seem to come over in Friedman's essay. But it is hard to pinpoint (he does remark that the law for falling bodies is wildly out for a feather, by which he probably means that the atmosphere is not near enough to a vacuum for a feather, i.e. the presupposition is not realised). Moreover, he explicitly says that to be important 'a hypothesis must be descriptively false in its assumptions' (Friedman 1953, p. 14). But in fact — perhaps by discussing so many points all at once — the point is not so much in evidence as he may have wished to make it. Indeed I think he *underplays* it. It is one of the most important ideas in metascience. Failure to grasp it has led to widespread misunderstanding of the nature of the most highly explanatory theories of natural science. Friedman is concerned with presuppositions that are 'unrealistic', do not correspond to anything in the observable world. These are what I call non-instantiative. It would surely help social scientists in general and economists in particular if they were shown that the greatest theories in natural science have non-instantiative terms — terms that do not refer to observables (gravitational force, electromagnetic field, atom, electron, gene, and so on); and that such terms are not tested for realism — the theories are tested by their consequences alone.

The reader will find most important clarifications of Friedman's essay made by Musgrave (1981). Though Musgrave and I would see the matter largely in the same way, he disagrees with the idea of unrealism of assumptions, because this would, he holds, necessitate giving the theory embodying them an instrumentalist interpretation. (I would not regard this as satisfactory either). On my view, the aim is to get a realistic theory which describes the real world, but I doubt whether this goal is often achieved. It is not because instrumentalistic hypotheses are all we want that I am satisfied with non-instantiative hypotheses, but because they have high explanatory power (instrumentalism is an initial step on the way towards knowledge of reality), and because they contrast with *observationalism*, which would require the terms of the hypothesis to denote observable instances.

Appendix 8.3: Reductionism

Reductionism is a *programme* and it has long been one. Our first objective is to find out its *purpose* and its problem if any.

From the Renaissance onwards straight progress was made continuously in the natural sciences, meaning for the most part the physical sciences, and this meant progress in understanding the material world. The great revolution that took place from the time of Copernicus onwards lay in the belief that causation could be firmly located in matter. When it came to the human mind, however, psychology was in a much weaker state and little or no progress was made. Mental phenomena gave mainly the impression of being chaotic, what James later called a 'blooming, buzzing confusion'. People were only too well aware of this if they reflected on the bizarre nature of their own dreams. It almost certainly seemed beyond hope for human intelligence to be able to bring order into this chaotic area. Moreover, from time immemorial, people were well aware of the effects that the material world could have upon mental phenomena. Thus, the effects of alchohol upon the mind or the effects of physical poisons were too well known to need underlining, not to mention near runners-up such as illness, particularly fevers. It was therefore natural enough to see the world in terms of material causation producing a variety of mental effects. And it was apparently not too difficult to overlook the traffic going in the opposite direction, to overlook that thoughts in men's minds and decisions taken by them had altered the face of Nature, or other phenomena just as noticeable such as the influence of men's thoughts upon their own bodies and the influence of men's thoughts upon the actions, including the bodily activity, of other people. The traffic this way was not entirely overlooked but it was overwhelmed by the opposite influences of material causation. And this was more especially, I think, because the advances due to seeing the world in terms of material causation had brought civilisation out of the Middle Ages into the modern world.

If the thought (an enormous step for the philosophical intellect to take), developed the notion of material causation from being one of merely very great influence, to being one of universal dominance, what this would mean is quite simple. It would mean that all mental changes in a person's mind were produced by physiological changes in his body — but also, that no events in a person's mind would possess causal efficacy at all and, in particular, effect changes in a person's body. With a statement of a completely one-way traffic of causation from the material world, and in particular the human body, to the mental world, that is, the human mind, we have a universal doctrine to contend with. It has become known as 'epiphenomenalism' — the term was, I understand, introduced by T.H. Huxley, the great Darwinian sup-

94

porter, in the middle of the last century. Hitherto there had not been wanting thinkers to maintain such a position but it was long before it received a name. Since its baptism, however, it has become an increasingly influential idea.

From the foregoing it is not difficult to see the purpose behind reductionism. It was to bring order into a chaotic field such as the mind, by reducing the problem to one of explanation in terms of the material domain, where at least progress had been made, which gave promise and encouraged optimism that more progress could be made. In other words, it would have seemed a more hopeful task to try to explain the world of the mind in terms of the material world than to try to explain it on its own, in its own terms.

If one seeks to replace this overall goal by the notion of a problem perhaps this could be expressed by saying that the world of the mind defeated the best intellects, and the reason for this was not that there was no knowledge whatever about the mind, but that there were no theories about it. There were no theories, even poor ones, to operate with. No theories to improve. So far as there was a problem, it was to explain a chaos.

The programme for reductions

The more materialistic-minded thinkers were well rewarded in some measure during the last hundred years. They saw chemistry apparently reduced to physics. That is to say, all chemical laws could be explained in terms of physical laws alone (whether this is fully the case or not may be passed over here.) This reduction seemed to be the strongest one. It has often looked as if biology could or would soon be reduced to physics and chemistry, but the case is much more complex and there would not now be very much enthusiasm about the project in any quarter.

Thus, reduction as it developed in the minds of intellectuals was the project of reducing mental laws to physical laws or biological ones and of explaining mental phenomena by means of physical and biological phenomena. Somewhat parallel to this was the natural expectation of being able to reduce the laws of society to the laws of psychology. Then, of course, if society were reduced to psychology, psychology to biology, biology to physics and chemistry, then our whole understanding of the world would be explicable in terms of material causes. The materialist programme would be completed.

Two encouraging factors should be specially noted. One concerns the reductions that actually take place in mathematics, which thus provide a most powerful model for reductionism. The other concerns reductions that take place in logic, that is, in pure or formal logic. Let us illustrate these. From the time of Pythagoras there existed irrational numbers such as 'the square root of two' which could not be accounted for in terms of the ordinary rational numbers which include the integers and ordinary fractions. Irrational numbers seemed undoubtedly to be numbers. They behaved in many ways like numbers and yet there was something baffling about them. They could not be expressed in terms of 'ordinary' numbers. For over two millennia this problem defied treatment. Indeed, no progress with it was made at all. Eventually in the last century, Dedekind (1969) succeeded, in a very short paper of not much over twenty pages, in showing how a reduction of the irrational to the rational could be actually achieved. And his method, slightly simplifed, is the one used to this day. What this might be said to mean to the mathematical intellectual would be that kinds of numbers that actually exist in our world are whole numbers and fractions, and that any other kind of number is simply a derivative or a construct out of these. (Indeed Kronecker said that God made the integers — all else is the work of man.) Thus irrational numbers were not sui generis — or a new, unrelated sort of number. That is a simple way of putting the matter if one wishes to speak of numbers as possible inhabitants of the world. Other similar ventures were successful, notably the reduction of complex numbers, involving what are misleadingly called imaginary numbers, which are compounds of the square root of -1. But as a model, Dedekind's reduction of the irrational numbers holds the palm. We should realise, however, that mathematics is full of this tendency. For instance, in very elementary algebra studied in high school, a student meets not only indices which are whole numbers but also fractional indices and negative indices, and even at that tender stage these can be handled by a simple reductionistic method. More generally, however, mathematics consists of reducing tens or millions of theorems to a few simple axioms or postulates or assumptions. These consist of a handful which can be laid down at the beginning, and from them all the other theorems can be derived, that is, deduced. This tendency is as old as Euclid, from whom we have the first great textbook of geometry, in which theorems are derived from twelve axioms to which, therefore, they are reduceable. The aim in most mathematics is to relate various parts together, which is usually a form of reductionism.

In logic the aim has been similar, to derive logical theorems from logical axioms, or to reduce logical theorems to logical axioms. A paradigm for this is to be found in that colossal twentieth-century achievement *Principia Mathematica*, but the tendency comes from Aristotle who did a great deal of reduction of logical theorems in his own studies, and in fact carried out the process both ways, for he also deduced theorems from the first principles.

The first great failure in this programme is indeed connected with *Principia Mathematica*. In that work Russell was concerned not just with reducing logical theorems to one another, although he was certainly also concerned with that, nor was he concerned with reducing mathematical theorems to one another; what he did hope to achieve was to reduce the fundamentals of mathematics to the fundamental principles of logic. And in this, it is generally agreed, the programme did not come off, nor is it any longer required that it should come off, because the relationship between logic and mathematics is conceived differently.

What I have been aiming to bring out by comparing the different parts of the programme is to show that, as a matter of actual historical fact, success has been attained in the purely intellectual or, if you like, the peculiarly artificial areas of logic and mathematics. In these areas it really looks as if reductionism is fully appropriate. It looks as if it is inherent in the nature of the whole exercise. By contrast, however, outside those domains, all other domains concern the real world. They concern *empirical* matters. And here there is at least a serious doubt whether the programme is capable of being carried out or is a reasonable idea at all.

Although the questions of reducing chemistry to physics and of reducing biology to chemistry are highly technical enterprises, a comment is in order. The likelihood is that nearly all chemical laws can be reduced to physical laws, but that certain chemical properties are of a kind that cannot be explained in terms of physical properties without in effect inserting into the physical domain the chemical property one wishes to extract from it. And the same comment would apply easily to the reduction of biology to chemistry, or to chemistry and physics, though there is perhaps an additional difficulty here. For the mutual interaction of processes in a biological phenomenon may well be something that cannot be taken account of by purely physical and chemical laws. Thus, even at the easiest level of reductionism the programme runs into possible difficulties, and there is no agreement that the programme has been fully achieved here. Failure to achieve it at those levels would undermine confidence in achieving it at the level of the mind, which is the real bone of contention.

It may seem strange that such an issue should be so difficult to settle one way or the other. It has been common for years to point out how ridiculous is the programme of epiphenomenalism, or reduction of mental phenomena to physical phenomena — how it runs counter to commonsense and all our experiences of life. But, of course, this sort of argument has no logical force. Much more powerful is the notion that mentality has evolved along with the other developments of organisms within the world, and evolves Darwinian-wise and has presumably, therefore, survival value. And one would wonder what was the survival point of all this, that is, why mental phenomena were enabled to survive, and were not simply liquidated if they served no purpose, or, more exactly, if they had no function in enabling the human species to survive. This is undoubtedly a very powerful point. And it is amusing to note, as my friend Alan Musgrave has pointed out to me, that of all people to propose the doctrine of epiphenomenalism it should have been T.H. Huxley, for he was the supporter of Darwin and therefore a man who might have reasonably have noticed that the mind might be expected to have survival value. However, there is a counter even to this argument. It is that there can be concommitants of survival properties that are, Darwinian-wise, neutral; that is to say, they do not assist survival, but they do not impede survival and are not on that account liquidated in the struggle for existence. So this powerful consideration also provides no logical force; and the issue is where it has been from perhaps Darwin's time or even from the time of Descartes.

There are two other domains in which the reductionist thesis seems to show a certain weakness. One is in the area of Darwinian theory itself. Unlike the earlier physical and chemical theories, the Darwinian theory of evolution is not normally interpreted as a theory about individuals but as a theory about species. The theory concerns the survival and evolution of species. But on the theory Nature is not interested in the survival of individuals, except in a very secondary way in which they are involved in contributing to the survival of the species. Otherwise expressed, the death of an individual means nothing to Nature, the wiping out of a species does (if the anthropomorphic mode of expression will be permitted). If this interpretation of Darwin is correct, and it has recently been challenged, then of course it would be impossible to reduce the laws about species to laws about individuals. Therefore the reduction of this part of biology, namely the theory of evolution, to the rest of biology could not be carried out.

A very similar sort of riddle is to be met with in the social sciences, where it begins to look as if, at least on some theories, the behaviour of societies or groups cannot be reduced to, or explained by, the theories of the individual members composing the groups. If this is so, then there is another great breach in the programme of reductionism. But it must be emphasised that the study of this possibility is in its infancy.

The problem posed by reductionism

It is now easy to see that there are many considerations that have tended to encourage thinking towards one or other type of answer. It is, however, easy to see that none of these considerations is decisive. It is not too difficult to see that ideological considerations, religious considerations, or weltanschauungen of the times or of the scientists involved have had a considerable influence on the approach adopted and the view taken. A great number of learned papers have been written on the subject, poking away at difficulties of one sort or. another, but naturally, in view of the sketch given above, they have not been in any way decisive. Why, then, is the issue itself so intractable? And is it something that we must learn to live with and leave for ever unsolved? The reason why the problem is intractable is quite simple. Reductionism is not a scientific hypothesis or scientific theory at all, amenable to scientific testing. It is, on the contrary, a piece of philosophy.

Apart from ideologies and ulterior motives that may make intellectuals lean one way or the other, there is an object of importance about the subject, for it can determine a great weight of research that is conducted into certain subjects such as psychology or certain social sciences. Clearly, if the epiphenomenalist's answer is right, then most of modern psychiatry is a waste of time and likewise a certain amount of social anthropology. Or else, if epiphenomenalism is wrong then these are reasonable approaches, while leaving it open that in certain cases the physicalistic, materialistic approach could well be used occasionally. However, a practical way of looking at the matter would be to assess the general considerations that have been referred to above and to adopt some general plan of procedure. The overall results of all the considerations would seem to me to weigh — not to prove, not to disprove — to *weigh* against epiphenomenalism partly because it is unable to carry out the programme. That is to say, if a man decides to go out for a walk, there is no way of assessing the cortical circuits in his brain to explain why he takes that decision. In other words, the programme is a tremendous distance away from its implementation. Reductionism in this domain is but a hope, not a serious expectation. Looked at in a slightly different way, if a man has a car accident we may wish to know whether he was drunk or whether he was acting out of a suicidal tendency. In such a case, we keep our options open. We allow that the material cause, the physical, chemical cause, might be the explanation or on the other hand that it might not be. We are prepared to look in either direction in so far as we locate the suicidal tendency in a psychological cause, and are unable to trace that to a cortical circuit or hormonal changes. Thus from the point of view of handling the man as a patient, even if the reduction were to seem possible in three hundred years' time, our present position is that we can act on the psychological hypotheses at our disposal no matter what the ultimate outcome of the possible reduction may prove to be. The dual approach affords wider possibilities for explanation and for practical action. Meanwhile, we may keep our eyes open for problems that epiphenomenalism, operating within the physicalistic approach, might debar from being solved.

Notes

1   It is non-instantiative in a way that does not come over in the vulgarisations of the theory, which water it down to the little boy's wanting the mother's presence plus wanting the father out of the way; whereas Freud's uncompromising theory is an unconscious incestuous desire for the mother and an unconscious hatred of the father. Now even if the popularisation were an improvement, as being reasonable and possibly true, and even if Freud's version were ridiculously extreme, it is Freud's actual theory, as historically portrayed, that I am concerned with as providing a theoretical explanation with non-instantiative concepts.

2   This lack does, I think, detract somewhat from the work both academically and as a textbook. A further deficiency noted in the original review is that 'The author has not discussed the nature of institutions.'

3   '. . . the only relevant test of the *validity* of a hypothesis is comparison of its predictions with experience. The hypothesis is rejected if its predictions are contradicted ("frequently" or more often than predictions from an alternative hypothesis); it is accepted if its predictions are not contradicted; great confidence is attached to it if it has survived many opportunities for contradiction. Factual evidence can never "prove" a hypothesis; it can only fail to disprove it, which is what we generally mean when we say, somewhat inexactly, that the hypothesis has been "confirmed" by experience.' (Friedman, 1953, pp. 8–9; cf. Wisdom, 1987.)

References

Brown, Robert (1963), *Explanation in Social Science*, Routledge & Kegan Paul, London

Dedekind, Richard (1969), 'Stet yhüt in irrationale Zahlen', *Gesamelte mathematische Werke*, 315–34

Friedman, Milton (1953), 'The Methodology of Positive Economics', *Essays in Positive Economics*, University of Chicago Press, Chicago, 3–43

Musgrave, Alan (1981),' "Unreal Assumptions" in Economic Theory: the F-Twist Untwisted', *Kyklos, 34*, 377–87

Popper, K.R. (1964), *The Poverty of Historicism*, London

Whitehead, A.N. and Russell, B. (1910fg) *Principia Mathematica*, Cambridge.

Wisdom, J.O. (1952), *Foundations of Inference in Natural Science*, Chapter 3.

Wisdom, J.O. (1987), *Challengeability in Modern Science*, Gower: Avebury Series in the Philosophy of Science, Aldershot, Chapter 13.

9 Are the social sciences value free?

The problem here is not at all easy to determine. It would seem to consist largely in certain confusions rather than in genuine specific questions. Nonetheless, I am departing from my general policy of not according a central position merely to clarifications which should hardly be needed; in this instance I am doing so because the matter has undue influence over contemporary thinking.

It was, of course, Weber who set the social sciences on the course of science in general in the sense of being inherently value-free. Opposition to Weber has developed in the intervening years, so much so that he is often regarded as an old fogey who should be put on the shelf, with this part of his work at least forgotten. The subject under consideration should not be confused with cultural relativism, which probably has a similar origin. Whatever else cultural relativism may involve, it certainly includes the notion that values are relative to a certain epoch or culture or society. It might be held further to include the view that theories are not value-free but value-laden. Here we have first to dissect certain different notions that might come under that heading.

The development of the social sciences brought about quite naturally and quite reasonably the discovery that many social ideas or intuitive social theories and perhaps some explicit social theories were socially biased — and to a considerable extent. What then does this mean, for it is not so unambiguously clear as it might appear to be at first sight?

Bias can play a part in determining what kinds of social investigations one may undertake. This kind of charge contains a certain fallacy in some degree, for it takes no account of a reality of scientific research, namely that it is possible to investigate only problems that arise out of the past history of problems and attempted solutions. Nonetheless, there is a grain of truth in it. Thus a social anthropologist, for example, might well have investigated the conditions that induced the tranquil acceptance by primitive tribes of agricultural policies suggested by their rulers. Now, it could very well be represented, and probably with truth, that such an investigation started out from the preconceived value assumed unquestioningly that the preservation of the status quo under the government was a paramount value. And the criticism might well have been made with some legitimacy that the investigation made no attempt to take into account the larger interest or values of the tribe itself. Nonetheless, although the value from which the investigation set out may determine what kind of investigation is considered worth doing, it does not follow that the contents discovered, either the facts unearthed or the explanatory theories devised, contain any values embedded in them. The discoveries made, actual or theoretical, may very well be objective in themselves. Thus, a tribe may very well accept a policy that would otherwise be unacceptable to them if it is presented in terms of some apparently disconnected value which is of particular importance to it. Thus, if the new policy can be shown to contain an activity that has been long recognised as pleasing to the corn goddess, then it may be accepted eagerly. And such a result would be an objective reality about the community which, although instigated by ulterior value requirements, would in itself be value-free in the sense of having no value judgement embedded in it.

If the reader should already be in some confusion, this could well be because the subject-matter has already given hints of values being contained in theories which are nonetheless, in a certain sense, value-free. How can this be? The possibility is not so difficult to clarify. Continuing with the previous example, the tribe may have the belief that the corn goddess will be pleased, and this belief is a belief in a value, or is the acceptance or adoption of a value. Now this value is part of the social discovery made. But the theoretical result is one *about* a value — it is about the value of placating the corn goddess — but a theory *about* a value can itself be value-free. What, then, is it to be value-laden?

To try to bring out the sense in which a theory might be value-laden let us turn to a physiological analogue. Is the science of physiology value-free or not? Many people would say that it was not, but this is erroneous. The study of the human body consists in facts, generalisations, and theories, about the operations or processes that take place in the human body. Now these may be good or they may be bad from our human point of view. However, for convenience we hive off the good ones from the bad ones and we call the bad ones pathology and we call the good ones physiology. So, in doing this, we artificially create value-laden sciences. We study pathology in order to know how to avoid the bad consequences that may ensue, and we study physiology in order to promote the good consequences that we want. Nonetheless, the bad consequences and the good consequences or the values bad and good, as value-judgements, lie outside the processes and facts and theories involved; these processes and facts and theories are themselves value-free although they do foster ends that are values. Thus, if we study the process by which malaria develops, this is a piece of objective science even though we intend to use it to prevent malaria; results may be expressed in terms of malaria avoidance, but the scientific content is a law or hypothesis or generalisation about bodily processes. In the case of the tribe, the objective content of the discovery made concerns the tribe's reactions to the value put upon the corn goddess and these reactions are the subject-matter of value-free laws.

It is worth underlining the notion that values and the social reaction to them are two different things. The values are determinants of scientific laws in an objective sense in so far as they evoke a reaction from a community. It is the community's reactions that constitute the subject-matter of the laws, but values are a hugely important social determinant in that it is because of society's values that many things are done. Such values can be components of laws about society. But this does not render the values, which influence an investigation, part of the resulting social theory.

These various distinctions so far drawn may help to elucidate the subject and help to show that the object of scientific study of a society may be conducted without detriment to recognition of values held by that society and help to show that the scientific study of society is not necessarily distorted because it is not wholly value-free.

One wonders, then, if there is any other situation that might be the source of the notion that values are actually embedded in the theories themselves. I think it is possible to find examples of just this. One might be the following. In the long history of mankind and of womankind, it has been well-nigh universally held that there were many activities in social life that women could not carry out. And behind this or perhaps embedded in it was unquestionably, I would think, the notion that a woman is inherently an inferior creature, a kind of second-rate man. Here would seem to be a case where the notion of a woman was part of the theory about what could or could not be done.

If this example is understandable and acceptable it is not too difficult to extend it and to see that similar attitudes have been adopted at various times towards numerous ghetto groups such as the Blacks, the Italians, the Irish, the Poles, as viewed for example in the United States.

Now here we have a really important kind of embedded value-judgement, and it is of the first importance to eradicate it and all such kinds of value-judgements from the social sciences. Nonetheless, it is worth noticing that the error involved, although a social bias, is equivalent to an *intellectual mistake* and one that can be *eradicated* as can any other kind of scientific error.

Viewed in these ways the overall conclusion seems inescapable that the social sciences, to be sciences, have to be practised as value-free even though certain precautions have to be taken. And that no human injustice need necessarily be perpetuated by taking them to be value-free. Indeed the reverse is the case. If we fall for the error of supposing that social sciences are inherently value-laden, the likelihood is that we shall make no progress with them.

10 On finding out what actually happens

If we are to do social science, indeed if we are to do science at all, we require at some stage or other some relatively firm observations. But it turns out that there is a tremendous task involved in making a social observation and we have to consider whether this task is so great as to undermine the possibility of doing genuine social science at all.

There is a very long tradition that the one sure thing that can be done in science is to make observations. This cornerstone was laid by Bacon about four hundred years ago and it has been believed ever since, at least by empiricists and scientists, up to the time of say, Bertrand Russell, writing in similar vein just before and also just after World War I. It continued to be a standard belief almost universally held, up to about the beginning of World War II. Since the end of World War II, the belief has faded away, disbelief being almost universal in the various schools, or some varieties of schools, that have arisen since then. Like many other contentions in philosophy — whether accepted or rejected — it has become a question of general outlook rather than of firm proof or refutation. That is to say, one cannot point to a standard refutation of the objectivity of observations. The view as it is now widely held is perhaps best expressed in organic terms, as it were, namely that observations are theory-impregnated. That is to say, that an observation pure and simple does not exist but is dependent upon some theory or other. This is sometimes expressed by saying — over briefly — that observations are theories. That as a mode of expression is somewhat misleading, although it is in a certain sense true; it is just that there is no real observational ingredient that could be separately distinguished from the whole, but there is an observational ingredient that coalesces with the whole so as to constitute something more than an abstract theory. The contention actually being made is that, whatever observational ingredient there actually is, is modified in some way or other by a battery of theoretical ideas that the observer brings to bear upon making an observation. Perhaps the closest model that one could draw upon to explain the reference of the notion would be that provided by Kant in his theory of perception. Kant, it will be remembered, held that streaming in upon us from a totally unknowable world are chaotic elements that are in themselves in no way perceptual and do not by themselves add up into any kind of natural object. Upon this raw material the human mind brings to bear an apparatus whose function is to synthesise the operation carried out, is one of synthesising this outside chaos — without of course our being aware of it — into perceptual wholes, that is, forming the ordinary whole object that we observe in the natural world. For those who do not find the model from Kant helpful, there is another one that can be drawn from gestalt psychology. As is well known, if we put a few lines or dots on a piece of paper we cannot, without very special effort, manage to see them simply as lines or dots: we see them as a configuration or as a figure. There are innumerable examples of this. They can be found in many places but for convenience I give one in Figure 10.1.

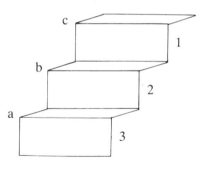

Figure 10.1

Although here there are only lines, they can be seen as forming two different figures. Most people at first would see the figure as a step projecting outwards, in which one looks from the bottom left towards the top right but then it can change and one can see it as a mantlepiece, from the top right towards the bottom left. And after a while it is possible to develop the knack of seeing it either way at will. Another way of expressing this phenomenon is that observations are interpretational. Or that there is no such thing as an uninterpreted observation.

Assuming, as I will here, that observations are theory-laden, or that there is no such thing as an uninterpreted observation, we encounter

108

minor problems for the natural sciences, but nothing insuperable or undermining. In the social sciences, however, the situation is far worse. For it can be questioned whether we can really make a reliable observation at all. To underline the force of this point I propose now to give a fair number of examples which I think are interesting even though they all tell the same story.

Questionable observations

1   You are in a nursery with some children and a storm blows up. Very often you will have no idea what has happened, that is to say, you will not know what started it going. Or, if you think you do know, you don't feel very certain of it and you have no means of checking up.

2   The situation was often, I believe, similar when Hitler accused the Poles of creating border incidents. It was, naturally, widely believed in the West that the Nazis started these incidents by provocation, and then reported them as set going by the Poles. There was no way of investigating the matter, however, because if a neutral commission of observers had been present, the incidents would not have started where the observers were but somewhere else. And it would not have been possible to establish what happened by enquiries made afterwards.

3   I remember a curious example when I was waiting to disembark from a cross-channel steamer at Fishguard. I was standing in a queue on the deck of the ship; the queue extended down a companionway, and on it was a family with one boy standing a couple of steps higher than another boy, presumably his brother. The upper boy held a newspaper rolled up. Then, out of the blue, he suddenly dotted the other boy a blow on the top of the head with the newspaper. That was all the observation that I could make. But as an observation it was useless without being able to find out whether the lower boy had said something to annoy the other, or otherwise engineered the incident.

4   It must be overwhelmingly difficult in many court cases to establish questions of fact so called. By this, I do not mean difficulty arising out of misrepresentation or deliberate lying. I mean, when different accounts are given by various people in good faith. One striking example could be taken from a fairly recent film, 'A Case of Rape'. In this, the evidence might very well seem to the viewer to be completely convincing and yet it was not so to the jury and the charge could not be brought home to the accused. And who will not know of cases of matrimonial disputes in which it is well-nigh impossible to know what actually happened?

5   When people draw on their imaginations things become still more difficult. I recall an episode when I was a small boy at school in Dublin. A friend and I were sent down to view the Remembrance Day celebration of the two-minute silence which was observed every

11 November at eleven o'clock. This was at a time in the early 1920s when there were still hostile attitudes towards anything British. The war of Remembrance Day was, of course, regarded as a British matter, although huge numbers of Irishmen had been in the British armed forces. When the silence was due to begin, somebody threw a small smoke bomb. An ex-serviceman jumped up on some pillar to quieten the crowd and assure them that there was nothing the matter, but, not feeling too sure, many people started to move away and walk rapidly or go at a slow run up the street away from the spot where this had happened. That, so far as my observations went, was all. But when we eventually got back to school, my companion reported the episode in graphic terms — smoke bomb thrown, wide commotion, people running in all directions, police charges (in strictness I should report that I do not recall what he said with the same accuracy with which I believe I recall the actual observations of what happened, but certainly they were to that effect.) I well remember my amazement at the dramatic and exaggerated picture he presented. I suppose it is an instance of the well-known trait of human beings to like to blow things up into a big story.

6   In line with this, or perhaps a mixture of two somewhat different situations, that is to say, a mixture of deliberate lying plus genuine confusion about what happened, is a highly interesting Japanese film shown a number of years ago. In this film, a well-to-do man, or perhaps a Japanese noble, and his wife were travelling through the countryside and at some point the man was murdered. The viewer is not told or shown by whom. It took place in the neighbourhood of a monastery and four men were found to be in the neighbourhood. The rest of the film consisted of their evidence, that is to say, of the stories they told concerning what they were doing at the time and what they saw. There was also the evidence of the wife. Five stories were all completely different. They were all coherent and reasonably convincing. The audience was left with the question totally unresolved. Here the question is one of ascertaining *after the facts* what happened.

7   Many examples could be given of historical episodes, some of which could be the equivalent of actual disputes in a court case. Thus, when the Irish Prime Minister, Costello, announced in Ottawa that Eire was about to leave the British Commonwealth, it is still not clear from various reports what were the actual circumstances of that event at the time — that is, the events not in the Irish capital in the cabinet, but at the press conference in Ottawa and before it, to which Costello made the announcement, continue to be a subject of much argument and interpretation. A similar obscurity can be found in the report of the Warren Commission, engaged on fact-finding to do with the number of bullets involved in the murder of President Kennedy and the direction from which they were fired. Another example would be that of

the episodes that came to be known as 'Bloody Sunday'. A parachute regiment opened fire on civilians in the North of Ireland during the 1970s. Here too there has been a Commission of Enquiry which has not left everyone satisifed that the observations were correctly made. If we go back far into history, it is notoriously difficult to establish facts in certain cases. For instance, was Henry VIII's second wife, Ann Boleyn, framed at her trial? Did Richard III, the so-called hunch-back, do even a small proportion of the terrible things he is alleged to have done? Including the murder of the princes in the tower?

8   A different kind of observation arises in connection with people's attitudes, moods, and so forth. For instance, one can get a report that he/she looked angry. How reliable is this?

9   Another kind of case would be: Does X (whom we know well) miss Y when Y is away for a long time? That is to say, are you sure? Are you puzzled? If you think you know, what makes you think so?

10   Are people sitting in a lecture interested or being polite?

Now it will be pointed out that some of these examples are hypotheses about situations rather than literally observations. But the difference between the two is not very great and one can shade into the other. Different kinds of questions can arise. In some cases this is a matter of not having sufficiently close observations made — insufficient evidence. Thus, one would think that it should be possible to find out what happened when Costello left the Commonwealth. Or to find out what happened on 'Bloody Sunday'. One would even think that it should be possible to find out more exactly what happened than is reported by the Warren Commission. In other cases one has all the evidence one is going to get, thus, in the film of rape the interpretation of the evidence can be argued about, the observations cannot be added to. In the case of the Japanese film, the whole plot is constructed in such a way that nothing further can be said. There is no possibility of cross-examining the witnesses in the film; the relevant characters tell their story, but there is no court scene, and no cross-examination by the police, and so on. Here there is nothing one can do beyond seeking for inconsistencies or unlikely ingredients in their stories. In the case of what may have been the deliberate murder of Ann Boleyn, one can hope for new evidence coming to light in the shape of diaries, or other documents. Where moods are concerned one can seek to test the observation by connecting it with the preceding or subsequent events to see whether something happened just before that would account for the person's looking angry. Or one could look for subsequent attempts to mollify and how these attempts were received.

In certain cases, like the assassination of President Lincoln, it is possible one will never know the truth, but this of course concerns more the instigation and backgrounds rather than the actual observation of what took place in the theatre. Likewise with prison riots there may very well be a total impossibility of finding out what has happened. In the interesting cases of storms brewing in a nursery, it is possible that with additional television recordings one might be able to discover a little more about these. It can be pretty firmly established that some children have a knack or a highly developed skill at making almost invisible flips which are known only to their recipient, making him look like the guilty party when he reacts aggressively. Some people report that these things can happen under one's nose. Thus, one is unable to see what has actually happened. The most that one may be able to observe might be a smirk on the face of the instigator, but even that he can learn to conceal. A serious practical matter that arises is what to do in situations where it is virtually impossible to assess what has taken place. In private life there may be some method of finding a compromise solution that does not depend too closely on what actually happened. But, in court, it is very often the case that everything hinges and is made to hinge on an assessment of what happens — and some assessment there must be.

The metascientific question that arises is whether social observations can be made sufficiently reliably at all to figure in a study of people and society in a scientific way. But there is no compelling reason to make the generalisation that, because some sorts of observations are highly unreliable, therefore social observations cannot be reliably made at all. The counter to be made here is quite plainly that a variety of social observations can be reliably made and everybody knows this. The only safeguard in discrimination that has to be made is to differentiate between the kind of social observation that may be unreliable from the kind that can be trusted. In practice, most of the untrustworthy observations hinge on unreliability of witnesses, a deliberate distortion of situations and evidence. And this is a practical matter which the practical people involved would seem to be fairly good at handling. When it comes to observations required for theoretical testing of social science theories, the situation is not nearly so desperate. Generally there are some difficult sorts of situations infected with a high degree of unreliability. Reverting to the case of the boy on the gangway at Fishguard, one might well want to use that sort of observation in favour of the hypothesis that the human animal is gratuitously aggressive. But that would be an idle use of the evidence without much more careful scrutiny of what went on before the episode. A most important piece of social investigation concerns the attempt being made at certain distinguished institutes devoted to the psychology of matrimonial misfits. Here is a situation where the investigators do as a rule like to know, and probably really do need to know, what actually goes on — even though in principle quite a lot can be done without being at all sure of these facts by means of therapy that modifies the attitudes of the parties concerned. It may well be that only after modification of the attitudes will the parties concerned be in a position to come out in the open and give an accurate unbiased account of the nature of the matrimonial conflict.

The outcome would seem to me to be this: difficult as is the task of making a social observation in many cases, it is not in principle impossible to make accurate ones, and so far as the type of observation is concerned that is required for the testing of important social hypotheses, such observations can best be handled as they arise. That is to say, when we have a significant theory to test, and have arrived at the nature of the observation required to test it, that is the moment to investigate that sort of observation for reliability, *if* there is serious reason for doing so.

Appendix 10.1: Historical construction, reconstruction, and the past

Professor Nowell-Smith (1977*a*) reviewed in York University's journal — *Philosophy of the Social Sciences* — Professor Leon Goldstein's (1975) book *Historical Knowing;* Goldstein came to York; issue was joined; clarification ensued; the issue was not resolved. Returning to the attack in *History and Theory,* Nowell-Smith (1977*b*) has delivered himself of an incisive but measured barrage (28 pages), which looks overwhelming to his team; Goldstein (1977) has replied (24 pages) in a beleaguered fashion. It is seldom all that clear whether his return shots are landing or scoring, but in general he conveys that, for all his precision — perhaps because of it, Nowell-Smith has been off the point, even if it is not made terribly clear why. This is controversy nearly at its best, but something has gone wrong.

What is the issue? Nowell-Smith claims that Goldstein views the historian's work as 'reconstructing the past' or rather 'constructing the past', providing a historical account in accordance with the evidence, but not *concerned* with telling us *what actually happened.* Taken in the spirit in which it is meant, I would claim that this was a fair account. Being philosophers, of course, they get into a tangle about the meaning intended by this. Leaving this aside, however, we may take it as an approximate account of Goldstein's position — that history is what the historian constructs — while allowing that it does not involve the wilder implications Goldstein thinks are being ascribed to him. Further Goldstein makes repeated statements of various kinds to the effect that, though something did actually happen, that is all we can know about what actually happened, and *what* actually happened has no bearing on the *historian's work*. Nowell-Smith thinks that *what actually happened* is what gives point to the historian's work. (I would say that a historian makes his construction in order to give a picture of what actually happened.) Goldstein thinks that some historians may have a motive of this sort, but that that motive is irrelevant. To summarise the issue: is the historical past a historian's construction or is it the past which the historian is trying to depict by means of his construction?

All the lengthy arguments end up indecisively. I wish to add a different consideration.

Goldstein's position hinges on the fact that if you wish to recheck something about the salt-cellar on the table you can; while if you want to check something about George Washington you cannot. However: you cannot check up on the salt-cellar as it was a minute ago, for that belongs to the historical past — you can only, à la Goldstein, construct it. So all we can check up on is immediate experience. Thus Goldstein has to be imprisoned in the present moment and be a solipsist as regards the past. I would suggest that this is a simple reductio ad absurdum.

(While taking issue with Professor Goldstein on this matter, this is no way impugns the quality of the rest of his work; on this I see eye to eye with Professor Nowell-Smith; I agree with virtually all the rest in Goldstein, but I think that history is a picture of the past.)

Appendix 10.2: The problem of the participant observer

There are felt to be certain problems in connection with an observer of a society or group who is himself a member of the group. There may even be a paradox in such a situation.

Some of the difficulties experienced are probably psychological or social in a perfectly ordinary sense in that they give rise to practical obstacles to carrying out the work but are of no particular meta-scientific interest. Thus, if an anthropologist goes to investigate either a backward tribe or a ghetto group of a different social group from his own, the first thing he has to do is to explain his presence. If he admits to being an observer, a student of human nature, a scientist, a sociologist, a social anthropologist, or whatever, he may be held off a little as an object of suspicion, not necessarily an object of political suspicion but simply as a stranger prying into the affairs of the people involved. He overcomes this by entering into the life of the group, taking part in everything as one of its members, but then the question arises whether he can properly carry out his observations.

While he can of course ask a few questions, in so far as he becomes fairly fully a member of the group, there are many leading questions that he is debarred from asking as it would give away his position as an investigator. There are two possible ways of handling this difficulty. One is simply spending a much longer time than would otherwise be necessary, so that in the end he finds the answers to what he wants to know without having to put too many deep-seated direct questions. Another possible way of doing it would be to take what anthropologists call an 'informant' into his confidence and play both roles. In this case it will be pointed out that he is expecting his informant to duplicate himself. The informant has to be both a participant member of the group and also a sort of investigator. He has to stand aloof to a certain extent in order to answer the questions raised, and particularly the more difficult ones may make him feel the need to reflect, cast his mind over what he has himself experienced, and in so doing to detach himself somewhat from membership of the group. When commentators notice the problem of the participant observer in the sense that he has to divide himself into two roles, and almost become a split personality, I do not think they always realise that the same problem arises for the informant or for the people as a whole if they should happen to be told of the investigation.

Perhaps the next question to arise concerns whether it is possible to conduct an observation while actively engaged in doing something. Human beings have an immense capacity for self-observation. In this way, an experienced car driver can observe what he is doing in certain respects in his driving while he is actually driving. Great numbers of activities would be equally easy to split up in this way, but about others a question could be raised. For instance, a violinist playing a particularly intricate piece might be quite unable to attend to the way in which he did it. Indeed, Popper tells a story about Busch, who was put in this position when he was asked how he played a particularly difficult few bars. Busch replied, 'Oh, it's quite easy, you do it like this.' He picked up his bow and fiddle and suddenly found he could not play it. Reminiscent is the old story about the centipede who was asked how he controlled all those limbs. He, too, said, 'It's easy enough.' But when he tried to demonstrate he became paralysed. Thus, there can be psychological limits to the amount of self-observation that can be carried out while we are engaged in an action, but this limitation may not be one of principle. Or, on the other hand, it may be that there must always be a certain time lag between the performance of the action and the observation of it, which would be not so much introspective as retrospective, even though the delay, the lag, might be a matter of only a few seconds or less.

Another kind of example in this area would arise if one was a member of a tribe which was participating in some ritual, in the course of which it was necessary to take a drug; if the drug should dull the higher centres, it might well be that it would be extremely difficult to observe what was going on with the cool placidity of an investigator who was not under the influence. It would be like trying to get evidence about what took place at a party where people, including the investigator, had taken a good deal of alcohol. What an anthropologist would do, I think, would be to join in a number of such ritualistic situations and vary his programme from taking the full dose of the drug to taking a half-dose, a mild dose, trying to find a level of dosage at which he would still feel part of the enterprise but without loss of his intellectual faculties. Naturally, he would also try taking none of the drug at all and simply making what observations he could of those who had taken the drug. This would be a practical way of trying to have the best of both worlds.

However, I suspect that the difficulty involved in such cases strikes home with some critics more because they have an inherent disbelief in the possibility of a human being splitting himself into two components of personality. Maybe at first sight this does seem a very bizarre achievement and intellectually well-nigh impossible, indeed almost a self-contradiction, but the truth of the matter is that we can and do make such splits. And if the fact is unintelligible that is too bad; we still have to lump it and wait patiently until we can find an adequate way of understanding how it is possible.

Another form of the problem takes in a moral component. It is felt that there is a certain duplicity in being both a participant and an observer, and that one cannot give an honest observer's report because, so far as one makes oneself an observer, one ceases to that degree to be a full participant. To the extent that there is full participation, it must falsify or render somewhat unreliable the observations made. I think this is the converse of the situation already referred to, in which the full participant is so involved in his participation that he is totally unable to carry out an observation. But by means of the procedure already suggested above, there would seem to be no strong reason why a fairly reliable set of observations could not be made by a fairly adequately involved participant. In other words, there may be limitations to a degree on what can be achieved, but they are only limitations; they are not strong enough to render the whole enterprise impossible.

Indeed, one wonders whether there is not a paradox at the back of people's minds on this sort of subject, which could be expressed in simple terms to do with a relationship between two people rather than an observer of a group. The paradox would run thus. One person can fully empathise with another, really fully, only to the extent in which he loses himself and ceases to be himself altogether. To the degree to which he reverts back into his own personality he has ceased to empathise with the other.

Surely there is some practical truth in this, but there is also a great deal of practical truth in the fact that people can be themselves and also empathise to quite an extent with other people. So the paradox looks as if it is sometimes constructed in such a way as to make it impossible of resolution.

In an extreme case participation of one person in the life of another might be like certain cases of two identical twins. When one dies the other may have immersed himself so much in the first that he automatically dies too.

The net result of these various considerations would seem to be that while there might be some ultimate paradox of principle that could not be got round, this would apply only to very ultimate conditions, but would not preclude the exercise of a large degree of personal participation and of a large amount of reliable observation.[1]

Note

1 If anyone has been seized of a rash analogy to Heisenberg's uncertainty principle, it is worth remarking on what this really is. While it does tell us that we cannot have reliable information both about the velocity and about the position of, say, an electron (putting the matter in rough terms) it does not mean the position is hopeless; it shows us only that a certain very small error cannot in principle be eliminated, but that a good deal of closely approximate knowledge is obtainable nonetheless. If we wish to try to make an analogy here, we might say both that there would be a differential falling short of participation which would arise from the attempt to make observations, and there would also be a differential lack in the observations made which would arise from our involvement in participation. And it might be that the differential failure in our participation and the differential lack in observation might together be combined in some way that could never be reduced below a certain theoretical minimum. But perhaps that is only a playful speculation.

References

Goldstein, Leon J. (1975), *Historical Knowing*, Austin, Texas and London.

Goldstein, Leon J. (1977), 'History and the Primacy of Knowing', *History and Theory*, Beiheft 16, 29—52.

Nowell-Smith, P.H. (1977a), 'Review of Goldstein (1975)', *Philosophy of the Social Sciences 7*, 315—16.

Nowell-Smith, P.H. (1977b), 'The Constructionist Theory of History', *History and Theory*, Beiheft 16, 1—28.

11 The present position in philosophy of the social sciences

The issues that ought to be alive in this field at present are perhaps slightly more numerous than those that actually are alive. A basic issue concerns differences of methods, that is, whether the methods of the social sciences are the same as those of the natural sciences; whether or not this is at any one time much discussed it is never far from the horizon and its head rears up periodically. However, in fact it is a current issue and on somewhat new grounds from what used to prevail: the topics that used to come up were centred on matters of prediction, generalisation, quantification or measurement of phenomena, and such like. It comes up now, however, because of the large number of phenomenological derivatives that abound, whether rightly or wrongly, consistently or inconsistently; some or all of these approaches insist that they should 'go it alone' and have no truck with the methods of natural science. They have undoubtedly, some of them, added to the richness of our knowledge of social phenomena; but it does not follow that a phenomenon previously known or now enriched cannot be studied scientifically, or that it is impoverished by so doing – this may be so or it may not be so, but the case had not been made out and the issue is wide open.

Two considerations may be deemed relevant at this point. One is the very central fact that there are many examples of social knowledge requiring and given a natural science formulation; these may be most uninteresting to phenomenologists and may be not of resounding importance to our knowledge of society, but for what they are worth they exist. Thus, if population growth continues to accelerate then there will be a major struggle for resources concerning food and fuel. In the absence of a national emergency on a major scale, only extreme measures can induce a population to accept a cut back in consumption. And if power is possessed by a group for the first time secretly, it will employ that power for its own purposes secretly or at least unobtrusively. With such hypotheses it is possible to explain a great deal of what goes on in the social world, and indeed, they are not all that trivial either, even if they fail to arouse the thrill that may be gained from the study of street corner sociology.

But this is not the kind of use of science (as I understand it in the natural sciences) that is at stake. Probably few phenomenologists, once such examples are pointed out, would refuse to accept the role of science in such areas. What they are more concerned with is the (supposed) inadequacy of classical scientific methods used in connection with phenomena that they are especially interested in. Thus, for them the behaviour of people in a village is to be understood not in terms of rites de passage but in terms of the encounter between an adolescent and adult man and the encounter between the adolescent young man and the adolescent young girl. Certainly we learn more about this from reading a novel as written by the greater novelists than we do from the more old-fashioned sort of sociology, but the question may legitimately be asked whether these encounters do not raise scientific questions about such cutoms as rites de passage. At least we have here a genuinely living issue. It lives not simply because some thinkers bring it up but because it is an issue implied by the social theories or approaches they actually have.

A metascientific word of caution may be mentioned here. If a new method of 'going it alone' can be invented or found, satisfying some non-subjective criterion of reliability, that would be a tremendous achievement and advance. The question arises, however, whether such a method is possible. Such a method is, of course, claimed by phenomenologists, but there is a doubt whether it leads to uniform results and offers reasonable reliability. It would however, be difficult to prove that such could not be done. But if no 'go it alone' method is as yet satisfactory, while we may continue to look for a good one, there is little alternative but to rely upon the classical methods of science.

Connected with this, or perhaps the same issue in another form, is the question of whether or not there are such things as explanatory social theories. If the phenomenological approach is for all sociological purposes somewhat weak, then it has to be noted that the approach from the side of science is also weak: for though it may be claimed that in principle explanatory social theories are possible and that the arguments against such things do not carry weight, nonetheless this scientific approach is weak unless some such theories can be found or invented; and to date there is an undeniable lack of them. The academic social sciences have produced none at all outside the field of economics. The only candidates there come from outside the field of academic social science, those of Freud and those of Marx, and most commentators who are brought up in the field of natural science tend to deny that these theories are scientific at all. In this form the issue is indeed a living one.

This issue can assume a further, somewhat different form. The question may be asked whether there is any limit to the kind of entity that can be brought in and embodied in explanatory social theory. In the natural sciences it certainly appears that there is no limit to the number of levels and the kind of entities that can be used for explanatory purposes. Thus, the generalisations or laws of Kepler to do with planetary motion are explained by the Newtonian theory of gravitation. That theory embodies a most extraordinary entity, namely, gravitational force acting as a distance, something that cannot be observed in any circumstances whatsoever; nonetheless, it pervades a most powerful explanatory theory. In its turn, the Newtonian theory can be explained by a higher-level theory, namely, Einstein's general theory of relativity, which explains the Newtonian conception of gravitational force in a new way by means of a new kind of explanatory entity. The theory embodying the new explanatory entity has to do with ways in which the geometry of space is modified by the presence of matter, again a most extraordinary conception but very powerful. There are practically no other examples in the history of science of an explanatory theory having yet another explanatory theory above, beyond, or behind it. [1] In this particular case, Einstein sought to look for a further explanatory theory beyond the general theory of relativity. If he had succeeded he would have produced a theory two levels away from the ordinary level of explanatory theory. In terms of an elegant way in which Woodger (1952) put it: observations are level zero, generalisations or laws are at level one, then come the first lot of explanatory theories, such as Newton's theory of gravitation. They are level two and this is the common level of all explanatory theories. Einstein's comes at level three, and the one he was looking for beyond it would have been at level four, and so the process could go on.

Now is this sort of progression possible for the social sciences? For those who admit the possibility at all of explanatory theories at level two, there can still be a doubt because of the following contention. Since the social sciences concern human beings, then the notion of a human being is rock bottom and it is impossible to go beyond the human being in explaining human behaviour, unlike the physical realm, in which the objects we perceive can be explained in terms of molecules, those in terms of atoms, and those in terms of protons, neutrons, and electrons. This point of view would maintain that individual human beings constitute an ultimate entity of explanation.

The foregoing consideration leads on to the other great issue of current theories. It concerns individualism versus holism.

What individualism means is that individual and social behaviour must be accounted for in terms of the actions, aims, intentions, goals and ideas of individuals and the consequences of these, hence, it maintains that institutions, social customs, and so forth are all to be explained in terms of individuals. This is both an ontological thesis and a metascientific thesis. The ontological thesis means that institutions and suchlike are in their nature constituted by the aims and actions of individuals. The metascientific thesis means that conceptually the idea of an institution and suchlike are either derivative from or reducible to the conception of the aims and actions of individual persons.

Holism is an extreme opposite of this in its most interesting form. Diluted it hardly affords a contrast. In its extreme form it is the approach that society as a whole, without the additional factor of aims and actions of individuals, is what determines the social processes of society and of individuals.

Although this issue has not been discussed very much of recent times, it is a genuinely living issue in the sense that it has never been resolved despite the most stalwart efforts of very able individualists and counter efforts by holists. It is thus an issue that is or should be in the debating forum, because it is implied by very cogent current approaches. One reason why it does not catch the eye and is not singled out very much for discussion is that individualism reflects the tacit approach of the western world, which cannot therefore think in any other terms. So much is this the case that the westerner treats individualism almost as a self-evident truth and in some cases actually does so. On the other hand, behind the Iron Curtain the opposite prevails. The holistic approach is tacit as well, of course, for Marxist intellectuals, and for them individualism is as unthinkable as is holism for those in the west, unless, of course, either party makes a deliberate effort to see things through the eyes of the other.

It is a most important clash because the future of the social sciences must in large measure depend upon the outcome of the controversy, so it should not be let fall into abeyance. These two approaches are so extreme in their opposition that it would seem overwhelmingly likely that either one of them must give rise to a one-sided position and therefore to theories of narrow focus, thus removing the chance of arriving at the most powerful explanatory theories. On the other hand, this possibility may not hold; for it might after all be the case that one of them was wholly true and the other wholly false. If that were so then the exponent of the false one would generally get nowhere, while the exponent of the true approach would get whatever powerful theories might be possible.

These two issues seem to me the most central of all; and other metascientific issues would seem to be derivatives and dependent upon one or the other of these. They would seem to be more important than metascientific questions usually are, in that until some progress has been made with them it is quite possible that little or no progress would be made with the development of social science theories with content. What we want in the end are accounts of society which will enable us to understand society, whether this will be in terms of phenomenological ideas or in terms of explanatory theories based on scientific methods. The metascientific issues, though, of course, interesting in themselves, are of importance as a prolegomenon to the empirical knowledge of society that is so badly needed. Sometimes progress requires development of empirical knowledge, sometimes progress requires development of metascientific enquiry. No one can be certain which is the paramount necessity at any given time. It is being suggested here that the metascientific issues are of paramount importance just now; however, this may be mitigated by the possibility that if a worker assumes one or other of the approaches and then in the light of that seeks to develop empirical knowledge, then progress may be made along these lines. Moreover, the development of empirical knowledge, even without discussing the metascientific issues, if such development were successful, would ipso facto determine, at least for the time being, the answer to some of the metascientific issues. So perhaps, after all, the social ball is in the empirical court.

Appendix 11.1: Popper's philosophy of the social sciences

Popper broke new ground in this area in his two volumes *The Open Society and its Enemies* and in his *The Poverty of Historicism*. These were first published about the middle and end of World War Two. They are quite unequal in the space alloted to philosophy of the social sciences. In the first work there are very few pages indeed explicitly devoted to certain of the subjects. On the other hand, it could be claimed that certain whole chapters are relevant, such as those which deal with essentialism, bearing both on the natural sciences and also on the social sciences. Indeed, the work as a whole has a bearing on the subject. On the other hand, detailed consideration of some of the fundamental ideas is very scanty. By comparison the short book, which is his other main contribution to the subject, is highly detailed. It originally appeared as three papers published in the journal *Economica* before being reprinted without significant alteration in book form. There was, however, a significant addition in the new preface, that is the preface to the book. Tilley (1982) has given a useful discussion of

The Poverty of Historicism, which, however, does not alter the position significantly.

In this appendix I propose to state the main themes and objectives. The reason is that Popper's second work contains several overlapping objectives and although the writing is extremely clear and the individual sentences wholly understandable, the book is very tightly packed and does not read with that ease that his writing usually displays. The main difficulty, however, lies in the mixture of objectives, which I think gets in people's way. The reader may see one objective but not get a balance because of missing some other objective.

The overriding goal of the second work is to refute the holist's doctrine of historicism or historical determinism, that is to say, that the nature and structure and form of society must proceed from stage to stage by inevitable laws against which the individual is powerless.

Two comments may be made straight away as a preliminary. Some readers get the impression that Popper rejects all historical laws. This is not the case. He is opposed only to laws of historical determinism. The kind of law that he rejects is the one that claims that capitalistic society must inevitably give place to a socialist society which, in its turn, must evolve into a communist society. The kind of historical law that he would regard as unobjectionable might be illustrated by the following: If a rebellion is timed to begin on a Saturday night when the custom of the country is for most men to go to the pubs, then the rebellion will probably not get off the ground.

The other general comment concerns the strategy of argument. Popper uses a succession of very powerful arguments. But if one asks oneself whether they singly or collectively succeed in the aim, one notices that they are convincing in terms of, say, a sophisticated commonsense point of view and masterly in having a considerable *undermining* effect; but that his argumentation does not, in my view, constitute a logical knock-out. It is perhaps a pity, for the sake of clarity in the reader's mind, that Popper did not make this clear. I think he sensed the difference, because the one addition made in his preface to the book form of the argument is of a logical character. Too much should not be read into these comments. Even if a full refutation is not forthcoming, it is certainly an important step to have presented a very powerful argument that at least shakes the position attacked. Popper may moreover have had in mind that his audience, as he envisaged it, would consist of social political thinkers who could be influenced by strong undermining arguments and who would not, like philosophers, be impressed only by logical knock-out.

So much for the strategy. Now the tactics employed constitute a very real and very large contribution in their own right; and the tactical arguments may be conceived as successful in the metascientific field, even if they do not succeed in the strategic objective. This metascientific achievement, being detachable, may fail to be recognised as an independent contribution because of being devoted to his strategic goal. In this work I am concerned only with the metascientific thesis seen as detachable; I have not been concerned here with the goal of refuting historicism.

The linkage, however, between the tactical metascientific arguments and historicism is so close that the effort to detach them requires a little care. Moreover, there are two distinct banks of arguments, and, although they are considered in separate chapters, the fact that they operate in opposite directions is apt to be confusing to the reader.

The first set of arguments is concerned to support the thesis that there are such things as laws or generalisations in the social sciences. The material involved there has been presented in part by Robert Brown (1953) as explained in Ch 8, appendix 1; in the earlier part of Popper's work the arguments proceed smoothly and satisfactorily, and once understood it is not likely that there would be significant objection to them. The overall position, however, is not one of establishing that there *are* laws so much as of *opposing* one historicist thesis that there are no such laws. As just stated, this contention is, I think, entirely correct, stated as it is in terms of the overall procedure; but it is misleading because, in fact, Popper does succeed in establishing the existence of generalisations and laws: after all, what needs doing is to produce a single example of such and this he can do. No doubt the various writers at earlier times had made a few similar points, but no one to my knowledge has proceeded so systematically as to take up all the historicist objections that he can find against the existence of laws and generalisations. In this, Popper has done a really thorough job.

When we move on to the next chapter we may well become confused. What he has just been attacking is the kind of historicist who claims that there is no such thing as law or generalisation in the social sciences in the sense in which these exist and are understood in the natural sciences. In the new chapter, however, Popper is concerned with an opposite kind of historicist, not one who claims that social investigation cannot be like natural science, but one on the contrary who claims that it can and must be and is: Popper is now concerned with historicists who claim to operate *exactly* as do natural scientists in the sense of being able to make social predictions. Quite apart from the point that it is questionable whether natural science has as its hallmark the making of predictions, Popper brings out a number of deficiencies in this point of view. For one thing, the predictions are not short-term, small scale and in a word humdrum; there are long range, large scale, and grandiose. This does not in itself invalidate them; but it raises a doubt when a method of investigation claims to be scientific but can make only large predictions and cannot manage anything on a modest scale. Although it is no part of my present purpose to go into Popper's detailed arguments, reference to the odd one may prove helpful. Thus, he considers that the historicist is misled by the simplicity of such structures as the solar system. This system enables physicists to study a few objects widely separated from one another and well isolated from outside interferences; so it can make very effective predictions such as solar eclipses. As Popper points out, such constellations are highly atypical of physics, and physics is very lucky to have a few atypical structures around that could make for simple study. In the solar system it is certainly possible to predict eclipses for hundreds of years ahead. But this is not the hallmark of physics, and the historicist, in claiming to be scientific, is aping a misleading feature of natural science.

Another attribute of predictions, as understood by historicists, Popper claims, is that they are unconditional; and because they are unconditional he calls them prophesies rather than predictions. By unconditional he means that no initial conditions constitute additional premises from which the prophesies are made. In this respect predictions are totally unlike those in physics or astronomy, where they can be made only from laws or theories in conjunction with initial conditions, that is, particular conditions prevailing at some specific time. Popper calls these historicist prophesies long-range forecasts to distinguish them from scientific predictions. So on two counts Popper claims that the historicist procedure here is not scientific at all.

I would interpolate a doubt about the last of these points; for it seems to me that the historicist does in fact use initial conditions. Thus, when he claims that the capitalist form of society must move on to something else he is doing so in terms of an evolutionary theory, but also the initial conditions would seem to be present and utilised, namely the state of the capitalist economy in a certain phase at a certain time. However, whether I am correct or not about this point, his other point would seem to hold, namely that the aim of long-range forecasting is not characteristic of natural science.

Although these two chapters in Popper's thinking point in different directions, there is a common bond between the two which indeed may increase the confusion in the reader's mind, since he has a criss-cross of similarities and differences to keep in perspective. I mentioned that the historicist is regarded by Popper as apparently aping the procedure of the natural scientist making long-range forecasts. More explicitly, Popper's view is that this is a copying of a *misunderstanding* of the natural scientist. If we return to the earlier chapter in which Popper criticises the historicist view that there are no social science laws, we may notice that one of the typical reasons for the historicist opinion is that natural science laws have to be numerical or quantitative or that the objects studied have to be susceptible of measurement. Here again, Popper points out that this is a total misunderstanding of natural science, for measurement is indeed useful when it can be carried out and very often makes a good science better, but nonetheless it is not by any means a hallmark of natural science.

With these two chapters concluded, Popper has tactically aimed at showing that there are laws and generalisations in the social sciences on the one hand, and on the other that the historicist cannot argue on scientific grounds for long-range forecasts (which he needs in order to support his view that the capitalist society must become the socialist society and so on). This last contention of Popper's must however be scrutinised. What he undoubtedly does show is that the historicist does mistake the nature of physics for example, and misunderstands the role of prediction in science. But this criticism of Popper's succeeds only in demolishing a misunderstanding or a mistake made by historicists; it does not prove that the historicist contention is false. Here we need to draw up a kind of balance sheet. It is undoubtedly powerful to undermine or indeed to show the total falsity of all the arguments that an opponent may adduce; and if we undermine all his arguments, that certainly weakens his position. We may thus be left with no further interest in that position; or we may take the view that since the position is not refuted thereby, it may bear further investigation.

Popper adds a top-dressing to these two main procedures of tactical and strategic arguments. Thus, he considers very briefly the Darwinian theory of evolution as having served as a model for historicists and shows that this theory can lend no support to that position. Again, the success of Popper's argument may undermine. He weakens the historicist position but does not disprove it.

Popper's most important addition to philosophy of the social sciences concerns his thesis of 'methodological individualism', which I have renamed 'situational individualism', i.e. the doctrine that all social changes and all social institutions are to be understood as the outcome of (not necessarily deliberate) aims and actions of individual human beings, and not to be understood as stemming from any social whole other than what is reducible to the aims and actions of individuals and their consequences. This important schema goes largely unquestioned in the western world because it reflects the general outlook of the whole of the western world though in different degrees, and will continue to animate the western world because it is the opposite of the eastern bloc Marxist schema, which is holistic; that is to say society as a whole undergoes changes that do not stem from the intentions and aims and actions of individuals independently of the whole. Unfortunately, Popper departs from his practice in almost all his other work and gives hardly any space or consideration to his individualistic conception and theory. It is true that in his first work it is also mentioned but again with scarcely any elaboration. Its importance is extreme because, if it is true, then the holistic view of society is deluding itself. If it is false, the western world is deluded. Or it may be, as some highly important developments have been, partially true and partially false; in other words an alternative possibility would be that society is in part individualistic and part holistic.

That in effect is the end of my disquisition on Popper's metascience of the social sciences. But it is worth adding that he has been criticised for doing nothing to suggest how the social sciences should proceed. This is from one point of view an astonishing criticism, because of course metascience is not obliged to lay down what shall be done but to understand the structure and functioning of science. Metascience and the philosophy of science do not normally contribute to science. These critics would surely not have expected Popper to have added to biology or to physics. So it would seem that their criticism was misguided and based on some misunderstanding. The most that might have been levelled against him is that it is curious that, for a thinker interested in so many things, he has not in fact been a little interested in delving into theories in the social sciences and trying to add to them. Although I have just pointed out that it is not his job as a metascientist, his interests might have pointed that way, especially as he has in fact done this in physics although he is not obliged to do so in that field either. Indeed, I would trow that Popper perhaps disbelieved in the social sciences in the sense that he does not fully believe in the possibility of getting theories in that domain, even though metascientifically he would argue that it is the right of the social sciences to have them. And I think my doubt is supported by the fact that his emphasis in the social sciences is on social technology rather than on social theory, even though he knows full well that social technology is as different from social theory as ordinary technology is from natural science theory. The suspicion voiced here turns on his great emphasis on *piecemeal social engineering,* which he puts forward as a counter to holistic planning. Social engineering means social technology because engineering is technological, so the emphasis is on *doing* things; but the emphasis is also on *piecemeal* and not on large. Moreover, Popper's approach would amount to the outlook that we can only modify society slowly and bit by bit. That certain sorts of change must be slow must surely be granted; but it may be questioned that all change must be slow and it may be questioned that all changes must be small.

But these last considerations concern the top-dressing to Popper's solid work in the field; and the inadequate attention he has given them in no way diminishes the enormous importance of the tactical arguments he has brought forward and, in particular, of his argumentation to show that social science is and can be and must be after all *science*. This is his answer to the general question, are the methods of the social sciences the same as the natural sciences? His answer is that, in the

128

fundamental sense, properly understood, they are the same.

Appendix 11.2: Why is economics a (relatively) successful social science?

Economics is well known to have fully-fledged theories in the hypo-thetico-deductive sense, i.e. deductions can be carried out which serve to explain economic phenomena. That is to say, economic theories seem to be testable by their consequences — exactly after the time-honoured manner of physics.

Such success is weakened by a plaint from an economist who points out that the predictions that test a theory suffer from a certain defect. All predictions in all sciences are approximate, and to that extent in error. Now the limits of error involved in physical predictions are fixed by some theory, so that one knows whether an error lies within admissible limits, and therefore whether a prediction constitutes a satisfactory test. But in economics Archibald (1966) contends this is not so. Hence there is a weakness in the testing procedure. That is to say, economics is only relatively successful. Still it is fairly successful, and more successful than the other social sciences, which cannot boast of theories fitting the hypothetico-deductive system.

I wish to suggest there are two factors that together account for such success.

One factor is that economics operates with 'natural' units — units of money — which move. This factor is a considerable boon in physics, where we have 'natural' units, whether atoms or units of mass.

Now this factor would be powerless if people pushed money around in an arbitrary fashion (or if they interfered with the planets by giving one of them a push, just for fun). So we have to consider the actions of people. If people were 'natural units' we might be able to have successful social sciences. But it would seem they are not — that they are too complex to be considered even 'molecular'. In that case, why does their interference with money not make for chaos in economic laws?

To answer this, let us recall the idea of 'economic man'. He buys as cheaply and sells as dearly as possible, in order to maximise profits (there is no need to elaborate the theme in various contexts). However, things are not so simple. Most men, probably all, violate the maxim of economic man. Some 'waste' money on taxis or an expensive car instead of using a cheap car or travelling by bus: some for comfort, some for status. These are the goods they buy with their money as well as food and a roof. Again, many go-getting business men 'waste' a 'surprising' amount of time chatting to people, and by no means always as a business investment. The likely conjecture is that they have to have a certain amount of social contact. Then social contact is a good that they buy with their money as well as food, roof, comfort, and status.

Do not these violations of economic man's precepts upset the workings of economic laws? There are two reasons why they may not. (i) The number of persons who thus negate the practice of economic man, together with the degree to which they do so, are both small; I would conjecture small enough to leave the workings of economic laws approximately as they would be in a society consisting solely of economic men (without a statistically significant difference). (ii) The actions that contravene the practice of economic man — e.g. status, sociability during business hours — are market goods, and therefore subject to the ordinary economic laws, i.e. the economic laws of economic man. I would likewise suppose that another assumption, that of a 'stylised fact', which Ward (1972) points out is false, like its ancestor Weber's 'ideal type', works well enough because of being a reasonably good approximation.

The reason for the success of economics is, then, that red-blooded men act like economic man, on both counts, to a good approximation. And economic man's laws are successful because the subject matter of economics, money-in-motion, can be expressed in terms of units.

Postscript: It is perhaps of interest to note the plaint of economists that they have no adequate psychology available, and that they would be glad if psychologists would remedy this defect. On the contrary there is no such need; psychologists could probably supply nothing useful, and the simplistic psychology of economic man, which economists, not psychologists, have invented, is adequate: because it *approximates* to reality.

Further postscript: My friend and colleague, Jagdish Hattiangadi, makes an interesting suggestion about relative utilities. If there are non-economic utilities at all — such as social services and special housing facilities for old people instead of gerontocide — these may have very low utilities (or rather disutilities) compared with the high utilities of economic goods, so as to be 'swamped' by them, and no discrepancy in economic profit seeking is detectable. Another way of preserving homo economicus is to interpret economic theory as setting limits to or constraints upon possible social activities which are freely open to us provided they fall within those limits.

Note

1   Another fine example is of molecule, atom, behind them electron,

etc., and behind them weak and strong interactions (making four levels).

References

Archibald, G.C. (1966), 'Refutation or Comparison', *British Journal for the Philosophy of Science*, 17, 279–96.

Popper (1963), *The Open Society and its Enemies*, Routledge & Kegan Paul, London.

Popper (1964), *The Poverty of Historicism*, Routledge & Kegan Paul, London.

Tilley, Nicholas (1982), 'Popper, historicism & emergence', *Philos. Soc. Sc.*, 12, 59–67.

Ward, Benjamin (1972), *What's Wrong with Economics?*, Basic Books, New York and London, 20–22, 99.

Index

sufficient, 40, 41
    antecedent processes, 53, 54
    datable antecedents, 53
Systemic need, institutional, 64
    societal, 64, 66

tabula rasa, 72
technology, 97, Ch. 7
Teggart, 47, 48
testability, *see* refutability
theoretical terms, *see* non-
    instantiative
theories, social science, Chap. 8
theory
    empirical, vii, 11, Chap. 7
    general empirical, vii, 2, 27
theory-impregnation, 12
theory-levels, 121
Thomas, 11, 20
Tilley, 123, 131
Trevelyan, 44, 45, 48
trivial explanations, 26
Truman, 23
T-type explanations, 66

ultimacy of persons, 5
ultimate limits, 5
unexpected results, 4
unrealistic presuppositions, 12, 83

untestable, 86, 87
untested, 86, 87

value-impregnation, 15
values, 10, 11, 16 ff
    and social reaction, 105
    as universal, 20

Ward, 131
Warren Commission, 110, 111
Washington, 114
Webb, 34, 45
Weber, 89, 103
weblike, *see* networks
Wegener, 63
weltanschauung, vii
what actually happened, Chap. 10
whether tell group, observer or
    participant, 115, 116
White, 40, 48, 51, 55, 60, 63, 70
Whitehead, 100
why-questions, 22, 23
William of Orange, 44, 45
Wisdom, 83, 86, 87, 88, 100
Wittgenstein, 24
Woodger, 121
worthwhileness, 17, 18

Yoh, viii, 47